FLY BY

FLY BY

STORIES OF CEOS FINDING THEIR
INTERNATIONAL INSPIRATION

GRACE HUANG

NEW DEGREE PRESS

COPYRIGHT © 2021 GRACE HUANG

All rights reserved.

FLY BY

Stories of CEOs Finding Their International Inspiration

ISBN   978-1-63676-936-3   Paperback
       978-1-63730-002-2   Kindle Ebook
       978-1-63730-104-3   Ebook

The plane icon on the cover was designed by macrovector / Freepik.

Dedication

To all the dreamers and doers out there looking for a sign. This is it.

TABLE OF CONTENTS

	INTRODUCTION	9
CHAPTER 1.	INTERNATIONAL BUSINESS IS JUST BUSINESS	19
PART 1.	**INSPIRED PRODUCTS**	**27**
CHAPTER 2.	TATCHA	29
CHAPTER 3.	RED BULL	53
CHAPTER 4.	VINTNER'S DAUGHTER	67
CHAPTER 5.	PAYJOY	81
PART 2.	**INSPIRED STRATEGY**	**105**
CHAPTER 6.	CRATE & BARREL	107
CHAPTER 7.	STARBUCKS	125
CHAPTER 8.	MOMOFUKU	141
CHAPTER 9.	CONCLUSION	163
	BOOK ACKNOWLEDGMENTS	169
	APPENDIX	173

INTRODUCTION

"Good artists borrow, great artists steal. . . ."

PICASSO[1]

Sitting in entrepreneurship class during my sophomore year of college, I started off bright-eyed and enthusiastic about the prospects of maybe striking collegiate gold by having a great idea come to me and leading my own start-up at nineteen. We hear of so many students starting their own businesses nowadays, I thought, "Why not me too?" I'm not audacious enough to compare myself to Mark Zuckerberg who started Facebook when he was in college and dropped out to lead one of the most influential and innovative companies of the twentieth century. But, I believed in myself enough to start *something*. As the semester rolled on, I remained enthusiastic, but my bright eyes started to dull when the realization slowly dawned on me, "I don't think I'm that creative. How do I come up with something that doesn't already exist?"

---

1   Dan Farber, "What Steve Jobs Really Meant When He Said 'Good Artists Copy; Great Artists Steal,'" *CNET*, January 28, 2014.

This question has stayed with me over the years, filling a little space in the corner of my mind and nagging at me like a browser ad that just won't quit. I thought that all the entrepreneurs I know of created something that didn't exist before: Mark Zuckerberg, Steve Jobs, Henry Ford, Huda Kattan, Tory Burch, Sara Blakely. Then, I realized I was wrong and giving each of these people too much credit.

Don't get it twisted. These are some of the finest business minds who have reached successes I can only dream of matching, but alas I was wrong about them. They're great, but even they aren't "creating something that never existed before" great. Myspace, telephones, Mercedes-Benz, false lashes, high fashion, and hosiery all existed before each of these founders started their great companies. These entrepreneurs didn't create something that the world had never seen before; these people reinvented and improved on things the world had already seen.

If these titan entrepreneurs aren't responsible for plucking things out of thin air, then you and I should both be able to let ourselves off the hook for that too. This is what *Fly By* is all about.

The way we think of innovation is too sheltered. Oftentimes, we think that inspiration must come from within, invention has to be completely *original*, and founder creation lies in the individual. We glorify the entrepreneurs who came up with it all by themselves. We think that success starts from ground zero.

Steve Jobs and Apple.

Jeff Bezos and Amazon.
Bill Gates and Microsoft.

Most other companies do not start out like this at all. Most other companies do not create something the world has never seen before. Usually, companies capitalize on the reinvention of things that the world has seen many times already.

Millions of businesses in the food, service, home goods, and financial industries also have compelling stories and lessons that can benefit aspiring entrepreneurs looking for their next Big Idea. And there is no better inspiration than a trip around the world.

When I studied abroad during my first semester of freshman year, I knew that I was going to have a great time. And it wasn't because I knew what experiences to expect or because I had a bucket list of things I was looking forward to in particular. Rather, it was because I had no idea of what was to come. All I knew was that my experience across the pond was going to be entirely different from anything I had going on in the United States. That uncertainty was enough for me. My goal for that semester was to come back with a broader perspective on everything: school, life, love, food, travel, and work. In London, I learned about another way of life. And it completely changed the way I moved about in this world.

One month into my four months living in London, I had pretty much perfected my grocery schedule, and it looked very different from how my family (and most American families) grocery shopped in the United States. My family goes grocery shopping once a week and hits two stores, H Mart for vegetables and Korean soy sauce and Costco for literally everything else. Why? Because my family prioritizes efficiency. It is more time efficient and cost effective to grocery shop at two stores once a week to pick up everything they need. Not to mention, the products are also good quality. Walmart and Costco entice shoppers because they sell everything at a lower price than most competitors. Consumers (including me) have rewarded these companies for their service by becoming loyal weekly shoppers and buying more things than we really need.

"More for less has been the best strategy in the history of business. It is the strategy of Chinese economy, it is the strategy of Walmart, it is the strategy of Dell, and now the company that is deploying this strategy more efficiently than anyone else is Amazon," said Scott Galloway, Professor of Marketing at NYU. "More for less always works because it is baked into us."[2]

BUT WHAT IF IT WASN'T THIS WAY?

In London, I realized that I was adopting the same grocery shopping strategy that I used in America. And it made absolutely no sense. Not only was I causing problems for myself by buying a week's worth of groceries that didn't all fit in my refrigerator, but I was also torturing my body by straining myself carrying all the grocery bags on my ten-minute walk home. One day after a month of this, I was again on my way to Sainsbury's, the grocery store in London closest to my flat.

---

[2] *Berkeley Haas Alumni Network*, "Scott Galloway—The Four," October 25, 2017, video, 50:05.

It was on this trip I said to myself, "It's only a ten-minute walk. I'll just come back in three days. I pass this place every day on my way home from school anyway."

So, I did. Instead of walking out with four heavy bags after shopping for an hour, I came out with two heavy bags after shopping for 30 minutes. My arms were thanking me, my legs were thanking me, and I was thanking me. With this newfound sense of freedom and literal less weight weighing down on me, I decided to reward myself with some bread. I was passing this corner bakery on my way home when I decided to walk in. They were selling a cranberry pecan loaf for three pounds. I was sold. I brought it back home and tasted it. Maybe it was the carbs talking, but I had an epiphany. *This bread tastes so much better than the grocery store bread, it's the same size, and it costs the same amount of money.* It wasn't more for less. But it *is* more for the same amount. It was a no brainer.

Did I discover something new? No. **I discovered something different that already existed.** British people have been doing this forever. This is one of the many things I was inspired by while living in a different country that I brought back to the States with me. I might still go grocery shopping at Costco, but I buy my bread from bakeries.

This got me thinking.

If nineteen-year-old me can discover a "new way" to do things, how many other people have become successful doing the same thing?

With the advent of Silicon Valley and the digitization of the modern economy, the world today is increasingly tech focused. It's no surprise that the success stories of entrepreneurs we learn about all sound something like this: Ivy League dropout eating ramen out of a garage pours hours into an idea nobody has ever heard before and, in fact, did not exist before. They get venture capital funding, and that start-up turns into a unicorn. The rest is history.

This is not to say that these companies aren't important or innovative. Of course, they are. This story fits into the origin stories of Bill Gates and Microsoft or Steve Jobs and Apple. Arguably, these tech companies revolutionized the twentieth century and have shaped the twenty-first century more than most other companies. But contrary to popular belief, these companies and these stories are few and far between. They make up a very small portion of businesses that exist worldwide.

Some might say, "Who cares? Tech companies are more successful than others and are better at raising money. The future is tech!"

I say those people are missing the point.

Dan Himelstein, Professor of International Business at UC Berkeley Haas School of Business, explained it this way, "I mean, we would love donut-making if you could start a donut company and become a unicorn company. It's not that we love tech. It's because all the money is flowing around tech. Literally, if you and I started a donut company tomorrow and we could raise money from Kleiner Perkins and all the other big VCs and we can announce we just raised series A round funding of $5 million for donuts, everyone would think donuts were the greatest thing in the world."

IF WE ONLY KEEP OUR EYES OUT FOR THE NEW AND THE TECHNOLOGICAL, THEN THAT'S THE ONLY THING WE WILL SEE.

This is the problem. We forget about the "donut" companies and non-tech focused businesses who also have billion-dollar valuations and the potential to be just as successful as their tech counterparts. For entrepreneurs looking to start their next business, only looking at one subset in an economy significantly diminishes the inspiration they can find. And if we only try to create something new, we may forget that it's just as valuable to improve upon something old.

"The rule used to be that you'd reinvent yourself once every seven to ten years. Now it's every two to three years. There's constant reinvention: how you do business, how you deal with the customer."

—INDRA NOOYI, FORMER CEO OF PEPSICO.[3]

Here's a brief sidebar about tech, as the stories in this book aren't all focused on it. Here's the thing: It's not that I think aspiring college students, business school candidates, and entrepreneurs shouldn't learn about the tech industry. Obviously, they should learn about the rise of tech companies, and

---

3   Adi Ignatius, "How Indra Nooyi Turned Design Thinking into Strategy: An Interview with PepsiCo's CEO," *Harvard Business Review*, September 2015.

they will because every college and every business journal are teaching and highlighting those case studies.

The problem lies in what they are not learning, what's not in the curriculum: the food companies and consumer good corporations and beverage industries that are also worth billions of dollars. Trust me, I would know. I studied at Haas School of Business in Berkeley, a city a mere forty-eight miles from Silicon Valley, the tech capital of the world. In my entrepreneurship class, I remember ten out of fifteen groups focusing on some kind of tech idea for our final presentations.

As I listened to their conversations, I wondered, "Why have none of us brought up the next big food idea? Everyone needs to eat. I'm sure that could be valuable too."

Himelstein said, "The more you travel, you realize that the world doesn't think the same way that we think here." It's this different way of thinking and living that leaves open the opportunity that entrepreneurs can monetize.

THIS BOOK IS ABOUT REMIXING THE EXISTING AND IMPORTING THE INNOVATING.
Through the origin stories of renowned corporations, successful companies, and innovative small businesses, I am going to show you that the way we glorify entrepreneurship is too limited. We are going to go on a global journey to peel back the curtain on stories of companies that didn't start where you think they did. On that trip, we'll examine the ways that companies shape and nurture their international inspiration to commercial success. We'll examine

the histories of companies that we see on street corners and middle shelves.

The world has been around for a very long time and seen a lot. To think that everyone can come up with something that'll surprise is an excessively tall order. But anyone can come up with a better way of doing something that is already being done or reinventing something that has been around for decades.

A CHIP OFF THE OLD BLOCK
In this book, I want to shine a light on these people and those companies that **got inspired, then imported, and successfully remixed.** It is not enough to assume that every company originated as an uncut gem when in fact they are a chip off the old block. We like to glorify the stories of uncut gems because they are novel and exciting, and that's fine. But we are also forgetting that's not the whole story. This culture of intense lauding of tech companies in Silicon Valley tells children and students that there is one true path of entrepreneurship. We owe it to our next generation to also applaud the stories of beverage empires and makeup startups that have origins outside the borders of their home country.

For all the entrepreneurs, students, and dreamers who have an itch for entrepreneurship or starting their own business, let's go on a ride around the world to see how the best before us got inspired to create and share their reinventions to make the world a better place.

CHAPTER 1

INTERNATIONAL BUSINESS IS JUST BUSINESS

"Every single social and global issue of our day is a business opportunity in disguise."

PETER DRUCKER[4]

Inspiration can come in all forms, shapes, and sizes, and at different times. But if you are an entrepreneur looking for a new idea, traveling is one of the best ways to do it. Why? Because when you go to a place you have never been to before, *everything is novel*. The food is different, people talk with a new slang, and cars may drive on the other side of the street.

For burgeoning entrepreneurs out there, going somewhere you've never gone before is a treasure trove of inspiration

---

4   David Cooperrider, "Sustainable Innovation," *BizEd*, July 1, 2008.

and information. You can find out about new products, new services, new operations, new systems of management, and new strategies.

And the concept of traveling to discover something unfamiliar and better isn't new. This time-tested strategy of overseas exploration has benefited our ancestors and society as a whole since the Silk Road. I promise this won't be a history lesson, but there is something truly beautiful about the idea of international trade that originated from the Silk Road since the time when transportation strictly involved camels and the years were counted by the hundreds. The Silk Road, ineptly named because it was neither a road nor made of silk, is more accurately described as "one of the most transformative superhighways in human history."[5]

Truly, the Silk Road was an intercontinental exchange of trade items: spices, metals, paper, glass, in addition to silk. The merchants traveling their specific segments along the Silk Road conducted an early form of international trade, which very simply can be described as the exchange of goods and services between countries.

They transferred one set of goods for another set of goods, but what made the Silk Road transcendental was the fact that the goods being exchanged were goods that merchants could not find or make in their native home country. For example, paper was invented in China during the second century BCE. By definition, it could not be found anywhere except China

---

5   Valerie Hansen, *The Silk Road: A New History* (Oxford: Oxford University Press, 2012), 5.

at the time. But when the Sogdians, a people "living in and around the great city of Samarkand in today's Uzbekistan," began to trade with Chinese merchants, "paper moved out of China via these overland routes first into the Islamic world in the eighth century, and then to Europe via its Islamic portals in Sicily and Spain."[6] An invention native to one country that is arguably the most important and instrumental product of human history could easily have been confined within China for another couple of centuries without international trade and the Silk Road.

The importance of international trade of goods, services, religion, and ideas truly could not be stressed enough. This is pivotal in the advancement of humankind back when cars, planes, and mass transportation were not even ideas yet and centuries were still counted in the single digits. If we think about it like this, globalization has been around for centuries and shows no signs of stopping now that international transportation has become exponentially easier since the eighth century. The only difference from then and now is that there are more options of goods and services that are traded in a fraction of the time. Instead of paper and spices, we now trade smartphones, cryptocurrency, and vaccines. Whereas it took weeks to transport one good from one side of a country to another, it now takes a couple of hours on a plane.

Ultimately, international trade was around far before we were alive and will continue long after we are gone. But, for all the entrepreneurs out there, there is an opportunity that exists now that allows you to capitalize on the scientific and

---

6   Ibid.

technological advancements that have come before us. International trade has evolved into international business.

PUTTING THE INTERNATIONAL IN BUSINESS

Now, international business is often thought of as selling a good or service in a different country. I'd argue it's not. This definition is so sheltered; it is only a shadow of what it could be. In this book, international business is everything international, everything business. In my interview with Monte Woods, the former CEO of OPUS Agency and longtime Vistage member, he said, "International business is just normal, and the world has grown small even if you're selling just in the United States, chances are you're trying to attract an international audience." So, no matter if we are talking about selling a good or service in another country, sourcing ingredients or resources from another country, incorporating a new idea, strategy, or process that was inspired from a different country, or selling something that exists in one part of the world in another part of the world, it's all international business. But, if we really step into the light of the twenty-first century, we'll quickly find that international business really just means business.

We now have a digital silk road that anyone can access to gain knowledge and information about things they've never known about before. We have overseas transportation that allows entrepreneurs to not only ship products anywhere in the world to their customers, but also import resources to create their goods or services. We have unparalleled opportunity to travel around the world and witness different ways of life and unique products and services that can inspire us to create something new or improve upon something old.

I got to live that last sentence out in my own life when I studied abroad in London for four months. I ate foods that weren't really accessible in the United States, like duck leg confit. I visited monuments and historical sites like Stonehenge that truly only exist in one place. And, I got to see how different British culture and life is compared to American culture and life, whether it meant being able to experience universal healthcare or open access to educational opportunities at the University College of London (UCL). When people ask me what I miss about London, or what existed there that doesn't exist here in the States, two answers pop out at me.

The first thing I miss is accessibility to valuable events. Let me explain. In London, I applied and got accepted to attend a J.P. Morgan Chase Women's Leadership Summit at Oxford, UCL Finance Conference, and London Law Conference. How did I find out about these opportunities that were happening in a country I just temporarily moved to and sponsored by schools I didn't attend? They advertised it on the Facebook Events tab. Then, I came back to Berkeley and realized how inaccessible our events are. It's not to say that these conferences in London were not exclusive, because they were. You had to submit a formal application that gets reviewed before you are approved to attend the event. It's just that these events were so much more accessible. Anyone can find the application to apply for the conferences as easily as you find a meme page on Facebook.

What would my entrepreneurial idea be? I'd create a service that event planners would submit their events to and attendees frequent to access these events. It would be a marketplace of conferences with free admission, and what would be traded is experiences and resumes. Oh wait, if I did this, I wouldn't be writing this book. I'd be the head of Facebook's Event page.

But I am not. So, let's keep going.

The second thing I miss are digestives, specifically the McVitie's Dark Chocolate digestives. This is a crumbly wheatmeal biscuit (read: cookie) covered in dark chocolate on one side. Throughout my time in London, I made sure to have a pack of these crunchy melt-in-your-mouth-delight-your-tastebuds cookies in my pantry as a snack. I even brought a pack back to the United States when it was time to come home. Unfortunately, it only took about a week for me to finish the pack and run out before realizing that digestives aren't widely available in US grocery stores. Why? Beats me. But what if I could make my own? What if I could optimize these delicious cookies and sell my version of it?

Instead of selling ten-and-a-half-ounce cookies the size of the palm of my hand, I would make smaller ones about an inch in diameter. It would be the perfect bite-size snack that takes the messy part out of a crumbly cookie. I'd keep the ingredients the same. After all, it's just wheatmeal, butter, sugar, and chocolate. But I would change the packaging to a jar or clear box that can fit nicely in any household pantry or counter instead of the plastic pouches. And lastly, I'd change the name to something more aesthetically pleasing and accurate like "chocolate covered biscuits."

So now, I have my product. And maybe, you already have your product or service idea too. The next question is where do we go from here? I say, let's start with deciding how to get your product out there. And to do this, I'd like some inspiration.

It's time to go on a journey around the world with founder CEOs and learn from the best who came before us. We'll be making our first stop in Japan to learn how Victoria Tsai unlocked a secret of skin care. Then, we'll go all the way to Thailand to follow Dietrich Mateschitz on his journey to solving jet lag with a drink. After that, it's quick ride to Morocco to follow April Gargiulo and realize that her experience with a facial oil and her wine-making background is a match made in facial product heaven. Then, it's all aboard to Ghana where Doug Ricket became inspired by the solution to electricity payments and extrapolated that to smartphones. Next, we'll go back in time and around the world to the Caribbean where honeymooners Gordon and Carole Segal found the key to sourcing luxury European furniture. Then, we'll go to the Northwest United States to follow along Howard Schultz's pivot of a lifetime. Finally, we'll end up back in Japan with David Chang taking his first steps to take his version of ramen around the world.

Entrepreneurship can be as scary as it is exciting. There are no instructions for founders and CEOs—just a seed idea and desire to see that idea grow into a reality. But I don't think that we have to go on this journey alone; we have seven founders and their experiences to help prepare us for our futures. Let's go.

PART 1

INSPIRED PRODUCTS

CHAPTER 2

TATCHA

―

"An entrepreneur tends to bite off a little more than he can chew hoping he'll quickly learn how to chew it."

ROY ASH[7]

Northern California. Ivy League Education. Worked out of a garage for the first few years. Got funding from investors. Made it big.

Who did you think of? I'm willing to bet some, if not most people, would jump to Steve Jobs, Steve Wozniak, and Apple. While that would be accurate, this is not a tech story, and this is most definitely not the story of Apple. Although, for some loyal customers, this brand's products are just as necessary as the prized iPhone.

---

[7] Sitara Abraham, "6 Inspiring Quotes from Entrepreneurs about Business and Life," *Thought Catalog*, May 30, 2014.

This is the story of a woman, her trips to Japan, and her desire to bring back centuries-old secrets; because sometimes, the best solutions are the simplest.

Victoria Tsai was a trader for Merrill Lynch working across the street from the Twin Towers when the 9/11 attacks happened. As life would have it, her husband fell seriously ill with an autoimmune disease right after the attacks. So, a day in her life in the following months would include going to work where the only view she could see out her window "looked straight into the hole that was left."[8] The harrowing view in front of her every day for months was across the street. Each American flag on the ground signified that the firefighters, police officers, and all those working through the wreckage had found another casualty.

Her weekends were filled with trips to the emergency room where she would worry about her husband. This all became too much for her, as it would be for almost anyone. No one would blame her for wanting to get out of Wall Street. "I don't know if I came up with it immediately, but I knew I didn't want to be there anymore. . . . I didn't want to be in Manhattan anymore. I didn't want to be in Ground Zero," Victoria says.[9] Eventually, ready for a change of pace, Victoria and her husband moved up to Boston where Victoria started to attend Harvard Business School (HBS).

---

8   Guy Raz, "Tatcha: Victoria Tsai," July 12, 2020, in *How I Built This with Guy Raz*, produced by NPR, podcast, 11:16.

9   Raz, "Tatcha: Victoria Tsai," 11:00.

During her time at HBS, she got an internship with Proctor & Gamble, an American consumer goods conglomerate. She was working on competitive benchmarking for SK-II, a Japanese skin care company.[10] What would be a dream job for most women turned into a nightmare. Having access to so many different high-end skin care products turned into using *too* many different skin care products, which became less skin *care* and more skin *harm*.

"It wasn't the brand, it wasn't the company, it was me treating my skin like a science experiment," laments Victoria.[11]

She gave herself acute dermatitis, a skin condition where the protective layer of the skin is damaged, preventing the skin from being able to keep out toxins, particles, and any other substances.[12] In simple terms, for someone suffering from acute dermatitis, everything is irritating. Her skin was so dry that it was blistering, bleeding, cracking, and scaling. Ironically, after using so many different high-end skin care products, it all backfired on her skin. Eventually, she was left with no other option than to use Aquaphor, which sells at most stores for under $20.[13] Aquaphor had its perks, but to top it all off, it left her face really greasy. She was frustrated by the lack of options. Desperate for a solution, she went to her doctors, who were of no help as they told her that her skin might *never* go back to normal.

---

10 Raz, "Tatcha: Victoria Tsai," 12:12.

11 Priya Rao, "Tatcha's Victoria Tsai: 'Love Your Clients, Love Your Products, Everything Else Is Icing,'" January 2, 2019, in *The Glossy Beauty Podcast*, produced by Glossy, podcast, 1:43.

12 "Dermatitis," *Cleveland Clinic*, last reviewed October 29, 2020.

13 Raz, "Tatcha: Victoria Tsai," 14:31.

After she graduated from HBS in 2006, she worked at Starbucks. She was a one-woman team flying back and forth across the world to launch Starbucks consumer products business in China. To be clear, she was developing and executing the strategy to sell bottled Frappuccinos in China on an accelerated timeline.[14] The job was tough. The hours were brutal. The one perk she got from all this traveling was layovers in Japan where she learned about blotting papers, which proved pivotal for her. But we will come back to this idea in a bit. As luck would have it, she also broke her arm at this time as well.

So, she was working with no days off, a broken arm that left her in a cast for months, and a monstrosity of a time zone difference, and she was still struggling with her skin problems.[15] In the face of all of these headwinds, she still delivered and had a successful launch for Starbucks. So successful, in fact, that Howard Schultz asked her to present in front of his board of directors about the project. You'd think that she was well on her way to corporate success. But she wasn't.

Despite all her hard work and tangible positive deliverables, at the end of the year, her vice president gave her a performance review that just said, "Meets Expectations."[16]

"Meets Expectations?"!

---

14   Raz, "Tatcha: Victoria Tsai," 15:36.
15   Raz, "Tatcha: Victoria Tsai," 16:34.
16   Raz, "Tatcha: Victoria Tsai," 15:56.

Victoria wasn't just unsatisfied at that review; she was offended. So much so that she resigned knowing in her heart that she would never be truly successful at Starbucks no matter how much she loved the brand and admired Howard Schultz.

Schultz found out and called Victoria personally, "Why? Why would you want to go? Tell me what you want to do. Tell me what job you are interested in."[17] The CEO of Starbucks was offering her any job in the company that she wanted, and she didn't say yes. Ironically, Victoria also had a contrived sense of loyalty to her VP, who was the one who caused her to want to leave in the first place. So, even after all this, she didn't throw that person under the bus and replied, "I just don't fit in here."[18]

After leaving Starbucks in 2008, Victoria was ready for a change. She was recruited to help launch a San Francisco tech start-up, GoodGuide.[19] Led by a team of scientists graduating from UC Berkeley, GoodGuide is a web-based app which created a tool to inform consumers about the sustainability, health, and social impacts of consumer products. With over 500,000 products rated, GoodGuide helps consumers find products they love from companies whose values align with their own.[20] As their first hire on the business side, Victoria was responsible for creating a marketing strategy and launch plan for the company.

---

17 Raz, "Tatcha: Victoria Tsai," 17:40.
18 Raz, "Tatcha: Victoria Tsai," 17:57.
19 Raz, "Tatcha: Victoria Tsai," 18:20.
20 "13 Years Ago," *GoodGuide*, accessed October 6, 2020.

It was here that she learned exactly what was going into the skin care products she was putting on her face and how those products were getting made. "What I learned is that we absorb about five pounds of chemicals through our skin a year. And if you are a man, you are largely going to expel it out through sweat and urine. But for women, we often keep a bit of it in our bodies; this is because we have a higher fat percentage. . . . When I started learning about the supply chain and the ingredients that go into personal care, I thought 'well no wonder I really messed up my face'; it was my own fault."[21]

Ultimately her time at GoodGuide was short. After four months with the company, she knew the spark wasn't there.

"I was becoming increasingly impatient with spending the hours of my waking life doing things that I didn't believe in or if I believed in, but it just wasn't the right fit or the right people, so I typed up a resignation letter."[22]

Victoria Tsai might have been on a very unconventional career path and done things other people wouldn't have, but whatever she did was whatever she chose to do. At this point, settling for a job that she didn't believe in was not an option. It was passion or nothing, and Victoria was about to bet everything she had on passion.

---

21 Rao, "Tatcha's Victoria Tsai: 'Love Your Clients,'" 1:13.
22 Raz, "Tatcha: Victoria Tsai," 19:56.

THE THING ABOUT BLOTTING PAPERS

At this point, she was unfulfilled and unemployed, and running out of her blotting papers. Remember her time at Starbucks? During one of her many layovers in Japan, she learned about blotting papers, which were the byproducts of gold leaf manufacturing.[23] As the Japanese gold leaf artisans would hammer the gold leaf, they needed a protective barrier between the hammer and gold, and this was it. Women would use this paper on their skin because it worked wonders taking oil off without ruining makeup or damaging the skin.

Victoria realized that she could use blotting papers to look less oily from the Aquaphor. Now, years later, she was running out. And, she couldn't find them in the US. The ones sold in the US are made of cotton, which wasn't what she needed. And no matter where else she went—Japantown, Koreatown, Chinatown—she had no luck finding these *slightly translucent gold- flecked abaca lea*ves

So, what's a woman who was reevaluating her life, her values, and her happiness to do? Travel. She went traveling to "find something to believe in again."[24] She ended up in Japan calling Tamako, her friend who worked at Starbucks Japan, to ask where she could find these blotting papers. Tamako led her to the gold leaf artisans, who couldn't explain to her why their abaca leaves were absorbing oil so well.[25] But they did explain that geisha were the first people who started coming around and using them for their skin care. One thing led to

---

23 Raz, "Tatcha: Victoria Tsai," 14:51.
24 Rao, "Tatcha's Victoria Tsai: 'Love Your Clients,'" 2:36.
25 Raz, "Tatcha: Victoria Tsai," 23:46.

another, and the gold leaf artisans arranged a visit for Victoria to meet a geisha.[26]

Let's pause. Who is a geisha? Geisha are high-class professional performing artists.[27] Geisha are referred to in Japan as Geiko and Maiko (*Gei meaning art, -ko meaning child, -sha meaning person*). Maiko is an apprentice geisha. After years of training in various arts like dance, music, conversation, and more from mentors, they are hired with a flat fee to entertain in an *ochaya,* a Japanese teahouse. To be clear, there is a misconception that these women are prostitutes. They are not. Geisha is a traditional, respected culture that dates back 300 to 400 years. Today, it is very difficult to be entertained by a geisha as it is a highly guarded society. It's not about money; it's about who you know.[28] Newcomers must get referred by an existing patron to enter an *ochaya*.

Maiko are typically recognized by their full white face makeup. Geisha only have to wear it on special occasions. And each have their respective hairstyle and hair ornament traditions based on age.

Victoria was able to meet a geisha at an *ochaya*, and immediately was taken aback by how smooth the geisha's skin was.[29] Victoria just had to find out what her skin care ritual was and was looking for guidance to cover up her own scarring.

---

26 Raz, "Tatcha: Victoria Tsai," 27:18.

27 Aileen Adalid, "Geisha of Japan: Understanding the Facts, History & Myths," *I Am Aileen*, accessed August 18, 2020.

28 Christina Liao, "An Inside Peek at Kyoto's Secretive Geisha Culture," *Vogue*, March 21, 2017.

29 Raz, "Tatcha: Victoria Tsai," 27:47.

The geisha then took Victoria and her translator, Yuko, to the apothecary where she buys her makeup. When they got there, Victoria saw geisha coming in and out of the store, and she remembers their skin being akin to a child's. It was remarkable. She thought if it worked for them, it could work for her too.

"So, if they reached for a bottle of oil, I would reach for that bottle of oil. And, then if they reached for a powder, I would reach for that powder," Victoria recalls.[30]

She went home with a magical box of waxes, powders, and oils. Everything that she saw geisha were using, she was going to use. Yuko wrote on post-it notes instructions for how to use each ingredient: "Rice Powder. Add water. Create a foam. Massage onto the skin or leave on as a mask."[31] In her own words, she knew she used most of it wrong, but who cared? In eight weeks, like magic, her skin was back to normal.

Why did she trust these products? She didn't really know what she was using or how to use it. Didn't she learn from her past mistakes about putting too much on her skin? Not to mention, she was pregnant at this time, so what she was putting onto her body was of enhanced importance. Ultimately, it came down to one key question that separated those high-end skin care products and these Japanese ingredients: Could you eat it? As Victoria learned at GoodGuide, those high- end skin care products just weren't that good

---

30 Raz, "Tatcha: Victoria Tsai," 29:53.
31 Raz, "Tatcha: Victoria Tsai," 30:18.

for your skin; it wasn't natural. But, *these* ingredients? It's as pure as you can get.

SHARING THE BEST

So, three years of dermatitis were erased with eight weeks of Japanese skin care. Her doctors warned her this might never happen. But they didn't know about Japanese skin care. Victoria knew she had found something special and wanted to share it with the world.

She went back to the gold leaf artisans and asked, "Can I buy these blotting papers and bring them to the US?"
They said, "No."
"Let me rephrase, how many would I have to buy to bring these to the US?"
"10,000."
"I'll do it."[32]

10,000 booklets of blotting paper. This was going to cost her $30,000, and she was broke at that point.

Later, when she went home to call her husband to tell him she just bought all this blotting paper, he just asked her, "How are you going to pay for it?"

"I'll just sell my engagement ring."[33]

---

32 Rao, "Tatcha's Victoria Tsai: 'Love Your Clients,'" 7:23.
33 Rao, "Tatcha's Victoria Tsai: 'Love Your Clients,'" 7:44.

And she did. She sold her ring back to Tiffany's on consignment.[34] But, it wasn't enough. All in all, she ended up selling her furniture and her car to pay for everything.

Over the next couple of months, she came home to her one-bedroom apartment in San Francisco along with 10,000 booklets worth of boxes, and if you know about housing in SF, you know there's really not that much space.

Victoria knew she had to start selling, but she didn't really have a plan and she definitely didn't have the money. That didn't matter to her though. She had a background in finance and knew people. Since the very beginning, she knew she didn't want to fundraise. Being near Silicon Valley and from her prior work experience at Merrill Lynch, she knew that private equity is about money, growth, and ROI. Everything is about money, and they don't really care what the product is. Victoria wasn't interested in the money; she cared about sharing the beauty and culture that saved her skin.

"I was interested in creating something that was worth loving," she said.[35]

So, she went to her friends, family, and partner and pulled together $1 million.

Money? Check.

---

34 Raz, "Tatcha: Victoria Tsai," 33:07.
35 Raz, "Tatcha: Victoria Tsai," 36:38.

Next came her brand name. She had been helping out Stanley Hainsworth, who used to be Head of Global Creative at Starbucks and is now Chairman and Chief Creative Officer of Tether, a creative agency he started, and she was looking for guidance on how to start a brand. He asked her what she wanted it to feel like, and she said, "I want it to feel like an exhale, a breath of fresh air."[36] Hainsworth came up with the name Tatcha.

He also introduced Victoria to Nami Onodera, who now serves as Tatcha's Senior Director of Brand Insight. "She said, 'When I saw the name Tatcha, I assumed it was short for "tatehana" which is one of the classical Japanese arts of flowering arrangement. And it speaks to **the beauty of simplicity in nature.**'"[37]

Victoria remarked, "That's far more beautiful than what we said, being an exhale or breath of fresh air."[38]

Name? Check.

Now, it really was time to start selling the blotting papers. It was September 2009, the middle of the Great Recession, no retailer wanted to pick it up, and no public relations agency would take Tatcha. They said "You don't have a story here. Nobody cares about Japanese beauty or natural or blotting

---

36 Raz, "Tatcha: Victoria Tsai," 35:12.
37 Raz, "Tatcha: Victoria Tsai," 35:30.
38 Raz, "Tatcha: Victoria Tsai," 35:50.

papers."[39] But Victoria still believed in her vision, so she decided to do it herself.

She had ordered labels from a winemaker in California, but unfortunately, they came misshaped. Pregnant with swelling hands, she took scissors and cut the tops off all 10,000 labels and packaged everything herself.[40]

At the same time, she started looking up editors of magazines and makeup artists she admired, and then she personally mailed blotting papers to every one of them, fully spearheading a PR campaign by herself.[41] Within weeks, she had a two-page spread in *Vogue* and a feature in *O Magazine* and the *Today Show*. Word was getting out there, but no one was buying product yet. So instead of launching in the US, Tatcha found its way to the UK. Space NK, a high-end beauty retailer, bought the first chunk of inventory.[42]

Most people would think to just continue on this path and sell the rest of the inventory in order to be done with the whole ordeal. But Victoria is not most people. Victoria thought she wasn't thinking big enough, blotting papers weren't going to *make it* for her, and her investors knew it too.

---

39 Rao, "Tatcha's Victoria Tsai: 'Love Your Clients'," 8:05.
40 Raz, "Tatcha: Victoria Tsai," 44:04.
41 Raz, "Tatcha: Victoria Tsai," 43:05.
42 Raz, "Tatcha: Victoria Tsai," 44:39.

THE ONLY WAY TO GO IS ALL IN.

At the end of 2009, Victoria was contemplating whether or not to take one of the two acquisition offers she got. Unsolicited offers had come many times before, but she didn't want to relinquish control of her product just yet. But, now she was at a crossroads, weighing her options. On one hand, she could continue the grueling and tough road of bringing the product to market by herself. On the other hand, she could get help from an industry expert for the tall price of equity.

One of these "experts" and potential acquirers even said to her, "You have lucked into this amazing concept. And, the question is whether you love your baby enough to give it to someone who is going to be a proper parent."[43]

"And it's like a shot in my heart. I seriously considered doing an exit at that point. And we actually went through term sheets. And then they left me at the altar," Victoria recalled in an interview with Burt Helm.[44]

With that deal in her rearview mirror, she decided to go all in and expand Tatcha's line herself.

She went back to Japan to find scientists to help her develop a skin care collection made of common ingredients like rice, green tea, and algae. The scientists laughed at her, "Why do

---

43 Raz, "Tatcha: Victoria Tsai," 1:00:16.
44 Burt Helm, "How a Geisha's Secret Helped Me Found My Company," *Inc.*, September 2015.

you like these old-fashioned things? Nobody will like this. Nobody uses this anymore."[45]

Her answer was, "Because they work. I don't care what's sexy. I just know it works for me."[46]

She went back to the oldest beauty book in Japan, which was written in 1813, and worked with scientists she found in Japan who also saw her vision to create products based on this simplicity of natural ingredients.

"The more we dug, the more we realized that the Japanese traditional approach to beautiful skin was not some sort of exotic flower that only grows on the dark side of the moon. Like many other cultures, hundreds of years ago, when women found that their skin was dry or patchy or breaking out, they went to what is in reach and what was in reach was what was in the kitchen. And the basis of the Japanese diet is the basis of their beauty," Victoria said.[47]

Her chemist incorporated the three cooking ingredients of rice bran, green tea, and red algae into an antioxidant complex formula called the Hadasei-3. This is the basis of most of Tatcha's products.

---

45 Raz, "Tatcha: Victoria Tsai," 50:50.
46 Raz, "Tatcha: Victoria Tsai," 50:47.
47 Raz, "Tatcha: Victoria Tsai," 49:36.

In 2012, they ended up with a skin care collection of four products based on the Hadasei-3™: "cleanser, exfoliant, serum, and moisturizer."[48]

With the collection done, Victoria needed to find the perfect retailer to bring her product to market. At the same time she was looking for funding as well. As an entrepreneur, problems don't come up one by one; in fact, usually they come up all at once. Victoria went through nearly every avenue of funding you could think of. She first approached friends and family. Then, she reached out to venture capitalists, being so close to Silicon Valley, just to quickly realize they weren't interested. She tried to get a bank loan, but Tatcha just wasn't big enough at the time to get approved for one. And then, she met with angel investors. This was her break. In February of 2012, she got angel investors to invest in Tatcha and they helped Tatcha land at their dream retailer, Barneys.

From the humble beginnings of gold leaf byproduct, Victoria Tsai introduced blotting papers and a line of Japanese skin care to the world. She found something that worked for her and bet everything that it would work for other people too. And she was right. From a $30,000 investment, Victoria Tsai nurtured her product to become a $500 million acquisition from Unilever, a consumer goods conglomerate, in 2019.[49]

---

48 Raz, "Tatcha: Victoria Tsai," 55:50.

49 Marci Robin, "Beauty Giant Unilever Just Bought Tatcha for an Estimated $500 Million," *Allure*, June 11, 2019.

Someone once said, "Follow your passion. Do what you love and the money will follow." Victoria loved her product, and lo and behold, the money and the success did follow.

Victoria's commitment to her consumers has remained the same even after Unilever's acquisition of the company.

She has proclaimed, "Our business philosophy has always been very simple: love your products and love your clients. Everything else is icing."[50] This is the kind of dedication that only comes from the kind of love she had that kept her flying across the world for years and sticking by an Eastern model when everyone said she wouldn't make it in the Western markets. It's the kind of beauty and authenticity that can only be found a plane ride away that makes Tatcha what it is today.

RETAIL IS IMPORTANT. WHERE YOU SELL YOUR BUSINESS IS IMPORTANT.
Tatcha is high-end Japanese skin care. Tatcha is not drugstore-quality skin care. How do I and millions of other people know that? Because you can't find Tatcha in your local Walgreens or CVS drugstores. In fact, currently in the United States, you can only find Tatcha in places like Sephora, the Ritz Carlton, and QVC. This is intentional. Sara Blakely, founder of Spanx, in her Pricing & Positioning Masterclass said, "When you are creating your brand, you have to be very clear on where you want to show up in the marketplace."[51]

---

50   Rao, "Tatcha's Victoria Tsai: 'Love Your Clients,'" 11:23.
51   Sara Blakely, "Pricing and Positioning," accessed September 20, 2020, in *Sara Blakely Teaches Self-Made Entrepreneurship*, produced by Masterclass, video, 4:02.

While it obviously matters that your product is in the market, or else you won't sell anything, it matters just as much or more that your product is in the *right place in the market*.

An obvious example would be that Tatcha wouldn't make sense being sold in a technology chain like Best Buy. Even if someone could make the argument that the price point of products being sold in Best Buy are on par with the price point of Tatcha products, this would be an example of bad placement. The people going to Best Buy are looking to purchase electronics, not skin care, so even if you throw customers the bone out there to buy the product, no one is going to bite. It's just not the right target market.

Another bad example of placement would be Tatcha products being sold in CVS. CVS sells skin care, and even though many consumers do go to drugstores like CVS to buy their skin products, it still isn't the best fit because the skin care sold at CVS costs around $10 and tends to be targeted to budget-minded consumers. Tatcha products are sold for around $50. The mismatch in pricing would mean that customers just reach for the cheaper product. Or, Tatcha would lower their price and dilute their perception as a premium brand. Neither of which are ideal.

In fact, when Sara Blakely began to create the Spanx brand, she had to decide on whether she wanted Spanx to be premium, mid-tier, or value based. She responded by saying "I wanted [Spanx] to be premium and I knew that by wanting to go premium it was important that I didn't address or try to call on anyone mid-tier or lower than premium *to start*. Because it is very hard once you do that to go up."[52]

Don't believe it? Just look at Tesla. Tesla came out with the Model S, its first luxury sedan, in 2012 and its second luxury crossover, the Model X, in 2015. Tesla took four years between introducing its first product before coming out with their mass market Model 3 sedan in 2016 and mass-market crossover Model Y in 2019. Even with these two mass-market offerings, Tesla retains their perception of being an overall luxury car brand because they started off with the luxury models. In *Kelley Blue Book Brand Watch*, Q2 2019 edition, Tesla was the sixth most considered luxury brand, its Model 3 was the top considered luxury model, and Model S was the eighth most considered luxury model.[53] Had they flipped the order of their offerings, Tesla's Model S might still be considered in the *Blue Book* as a luxury model, but its overall brand might not have the same premium "feel."

So ultimately, it is about where you want your product to be and how you want your customers to perceive you. To get this placement and proper brand perception correct, it takes careful planning as to *what* products you want to put in which retailer and *when* you want to place them in the retailer.

As if spinning the wheel back to 2009, Victoria found herself ready to go with the inventory and a ton of money invested

---

52 Blakely, "Pricing and Positioning," 4:25.
53 Kelley Blue Book, *Kelley Blue Book Brand Watch: Luxury Segment Topline Report* (Irvine, CA, 2019).

with no buyers. Retailers just didn't get her vision, "What is your technology angle? I don't get it."[54] At the time, Asian skin care simply wasn't cool yet. And back then, people were chasing the newest technology, the newest protein, the newest peptide. But, this simply wasn't what Tatcha was about. It wasn't based on the new, it was based on old. The whole basis of Tatcha's skin care line is that you don't need new technology to fix the same old common problems; you just need to reach into the simple and pure.

Victoria needed a retailer who would allow her the chance to not just sell her unique product, but also share its story. She was entering a crowded market but with a product unlike any other. To gain customer attention and trust, her story about geisha and traditional Japanese skin care needed to be told. When Victoria was able to land Tatcha at their dream retailer, Barneys, she found the perfect retailer who sold products at the quality and price point Tatcha products belonged to and attracted customers who saw Barneys as *their* place to buy skin care products.

Victoria explains, "One of our investors went to our dream retailer and said, 'Please give this brand a chance. And, if for any reason their products don't sell, I will personally buy back the inventory.' I will never forget that. It's the only reason why we ever got our chance."[55] Victoria knew the importance of placement and attributed part of Tatcha's success to her break in Barneys.

---

54 Burt Helm, "How a Geisha's Secret Helped Me Found My Company," *Inc.*, September 2015.
55 Ibid.

In fact, Dr. Geoffrey G. Jones, the Isidor Straus Professor of Business History, and Faculty Chair of the Harvard Business School's Business History Initiative, identified two factors as to why Barneys was a key retailer for Tatcha. He wrote in his Harvard Business School Case, "Barneys [is] the ultimate stamp of approval in luxury retail in the US" and "Barneys was also a destination that luxury retailers from around the world visited for new products and trends."[56] The reason that Barneys was so important is not just because it matched her target market perfectly, the high-end customer. It was also because they gave her the chance to develop educational materials like cards and displays that were necessary to really show customers what made Tatcha different, as well as showcase their Japanese backstory. For a company that was selling a dream no one in the United States had ever even thought about, this truly was groundbreaking. Barneys provided Tatcha the perfect place to sell to their target market and the resources to share the story of Japanese skin care all over the country.

Then, Victoria made her way to QVC, a television network that specializes in televised home shopping. This was yet another practical opportunity for Victoria to share with the ninety-five million TVs QVC broadcasts to what Tatcha is all about.[57] While on QVC, she has the time to explain Hada-sei-3, explain the inspiration, explain the magic. They also reached a whole new market of women who need great skin care but don't frequent department stores. In 2014, Tatcha

---

56 Geoffrey G. Jones and Veronica Tang, "Tatcha: Marketing the Beauty Secrets of Japanese Geisha," *Harvard Business Review*, June 21, 2016.
57 Rao, "Tatcha's Victoria Tsai: 'Love Your Clients,'" 12:10.

was a breakout star on QVC. It had extra positive implications that QVC placement also doubled as an ad. Victoria was able to grab the attention of millions of consumers who would otherwise never hear about Tatcha and was able to share the value of Tatcha directly. She was speaking to consumers through the TV and controlling her message, which set the tone for Tatcha in the very best way.

Lastly, Tatcha's most recent partner is Sephora, who took everything to the next level in the US and Canada. "Because of the fact that it is open sell, we don't have our own salespeople in there. And their cast members, the men and women who work in the stores, aren't compensated based on selling certain things. They are honest, their educational knowledge is phenomenal. I can walk into any Sephora store and they can tell me about our products and our brand better than anybody. And it's a very democratic place for people to discover and learn and play," Victoria raves.[58] Sephora allows Tatcha to reach a much younger audience who don't just buy the first product they see, but truly care about where the product comes from and what it can do for your skin.

I believe that everything that your company, your start-up, or your product is a part of or does reflects back on your brand. It's not just the sales rep or president who is the "face" of the brand anymore; it is everything your business is a part of. It matters that if your product is a luxury good, you sell at a retailer who sells luxury goods. It matters that if you want your customers to perceive your brand as being high quality, you show them through your production processes

---

58   Rao, "Tatcha's Victoria Tsai: 'Love Your Clients,'" 12:39.

in addition to your marketing and your ads. It matters that if you have a story, you let your customers know it. Your product is not what you think it is; your product is what your customers think it is. As entrepreneurs, it is your job to guide your customers to believe the message you want them to believe.

CHAPTER 3

RED BULL

―

Marketing is no longer about the stuff that you make, but the stories that you tell.

SETH GODIN[59]

Entrepreneurs aren't all twenty-year-olds eating instant noodles in their college dorms. Sometimes, they are in their thirties. Dietrich Mateschitz was thirty-eight when he came across his big idea. This is the story of a slim can with the logo of two bulls and the person who redefined marketing and embodied differentiation. We might think that eccentric marketing plans are the norm now, but this certainly wasn't the norm decades ago. However, to explain Red Bull's success, it's important that we start from the beginning with its founder.

Before Red Bull was Red Bull, Dietrich Mateschitz was Dietrich Mateschitz, a man who said, "We believe in creativity,

---

59 John Souza, "10 Best Quotes from Seth Godin on PR and Marketing," *Social Media Impact*, April 10, 2014.

we believe that everything can be questioned. Taking a few risks doesn't matter because as long as you are healthy, you have a clear mind, bright eyes, and two arms and legs, what can happen?"[60] Did he always have this kind of attitude? Yes.

Dietrich Mateschitz was born in 1944 in the small village of St. Marein, Austria. Growing up in this small town with a population of around 2,500 people, he was itching to get out and see the world behind the snowy mountains and rolling green hills. From an early age he showed initiative and great sales skills as he convinced his mother to let him attend school farther away in Vienna, rather than the university in nearby Graz.

In one of the only interviews he ever gave, he said to NBC, "I chose the university for the city, not for the university. But I could only find one course which wasn't available at Graz, which was ship construction. So, I convinced her that I had only one desire in life, and that was to become a ship engineer."[61]

He did not turn out to become a ship engineer. However, he did work as a ski instructor through college. It took him ten years to graduate from the University of Commerce in Vienna, but it wasn't for lack of ability. "I changed universities a lot of times," he says. "You know, it's a good time, so you shouldn't shorten it unnecessarily. But I picked up afterwards." What changed? "That's easy. When you are a

---

60 Sholto Byrnes, "Dietrich Mateschitz: Raging Bull," *The Independent*, accessed July 19, 2020.
61 Duff McDonald, "Red Bull's Billionaire Maniac Becomes a Media Mogul," *NBC News*, accessed July 19, 2020.

student and you are a tour guide in the summer and a skiing instructor [in winter], this is okay when you are 23, 24, 25. But a student ski instructor at 28, 30? It's not so funny anymore. Sooner or later, you have to decide what you are going to do. So I decided to finish as quickly as possible."[62]

He graduated at twenty-eight and began working for Blendax, a German company, as their director of international marketing. He sold toothpaste for Blendax for ten years. While it allowed him the privilege of traveling around the world, it wasn't enough. "All I could see was the same grey aeroplanes, the same grey suits, the same grey faces. All the hotel bars looked the same, and so did the women in them. I asked myself whether I wanted to spend the next decade as I'd spent the previous one."[63]

UNEXPECTED DESTINATION

He was looking for excitement, an opportunity. He found it in Thailand. Mateschitz loved traveling but he hated how tired he was after he got off long flights. One day on a routine business trip, he was sitting in a taxi after a long flight to Thailand with bags under his eyes, yawning. Whether he was tired of living out of a suitcase, tired from jet lag, or both, it didn't matter. His taxi driver could tell this guy was exhausted. So, the driver offered Mateschitz a drink from a brown glass bottle, Krating Daeng. He explained that this drink was all the rage for rickshaw drivers who worked nights and laborers who worked long hours during the day.

---

62   Byrnes, "Dietrich Mateschitz: Raging Bull."
63   McDonald, "Red Bull's Billionaire."

Mateschitz didn't have anything to lose, so he gave it try. It was sickeningly sweet, but it did the trick. Almost immediately, Mateschitz's jet lag melted away and he felt rejuvenated. More importantly, he was hooked.

Krating Daeng is a non-carbonated energy drink, created and originally marketed by Thai businessman Chaleo Yoovidhya. In fact, Krating Daeng is based on a Japanese energizing tonic called Lipovitan D, which was a vitamin and caffeine fortified beverage. Lipovitan D was originally marketed in Japan to business executives who wanted the energy to do more; Krating Daeng shifted its target market to everyday laborers and drivers. And, Yoovidhya added a couple of ingredients. Krating Daeng contains Taurine, inositol, vitamin B, caffeine, water, and sugar. It is a specially formulated drink designed by Yoovidhya and his pharmaceutical company TC Pharmaceuticals in the 1960s.[64]

Each of the ingredients served a purpose which was "synthesizing" energy. He used water because this was meant to be a drink. Sugar was used because it was a readily available cheap ingredient which made the drink tasty. Caffeine because it is a well-known central nervous system stimulant which enhances physical energy and metabolism. Vitamin B because these are the micronutrients that the body needs to convert food into energy. Inositol, which is a carbohydrate found naturally in muscles which can have a mood-stabilizing effect.[65] And, the most interesting ingredient is taurine,

---

64 Kristy Coetzee, "Krating Daeng: Thailand's Original Red Bull Energy Drink," *Slumber Party Hostels*, accessed August 30, 2020.

65 Ibid.

an amino acid which works as an antioxidant and stabilizer, and enhances the caffeine stimulant.[66] Together, they make up a very sweet and very effective energy drink that was and continues to be widely circulated in Southeast Asia. This is also the basis of Red Bull worldwide.

In 1984, Mateschitz was sitting at a bar at the Mandarin Oriental in Hong Kong when he decided he would quit his job, follow his dream, and become an entrepreneur. He felt in his bones that this energy drink was the next big thing. It solved his problem of lethargy and jet lag, and he knew if other people tried it, they would be hooked too. I mean, a drink that allows you to stay up for more hours of the day is every college student's dream. And that's only the beginning of a list of target markets willing to pay a premium for "extra time." At age thirty-eight, Mateschitz decided he wanted to start a company selling Krating Daeng in the West. He approached Yoovidhya, who had previously worked with Blendax, with a proposal that was sure to be exciting, and profitable, for both of them. This type of energy drink didn't exist in the West, but Mateschitz believed that where there wasn't a market, he could create one. The two of them each put up $500,000 for a 49 percent stake in the company, with the last 2 percent for Chaleo Yoovidhya's son.[67]

However, from the get-go, Mateschitz knew he couldn't bring the product to Europe or America as it was. The name of the drink was something Western consumers couldn't wrap

---

66 Rudy Mawer, "What Is Taurine? Benefits, Side Effects and More," *Healthline*, accessed July 23, 2020.

67 McDonald, "Red Bull's Billionaire."

their tongues around. Plus, it was way too sweet for their palettes. The first change Mateschitz made was to carbonate the drink. This was easy. The second change, branding, was a bit more difficult.

BUILDING THE BRAND

Mateschitz returned to Austria to find a logo and slogan that conveyed the unique product that this energy drink would be. Red Bull wasn't, and isn't, meant to compete with any of the heavy hitter drink companies like Coke or Pepsi. Mateschitz didn't have the money to do that, nor did he think that was the right way to go. It was never supposed to taste better than soda or be more natural than juice. It was a new drink in a category of its own predicated on what it can do: give the drinker energy. Red Bull is the original energy drink introduced in the European and American market, as we know now. But, in the beginning, Mateschitz was working on carving out a new industry with a new product and he was struggling with the messaging.

Mateschitz called up the only man he knew who would be up for the job, Johannes Kastner, a friend from his university. After graduation, Johannes founded the Kastner Agency, an independent creative ad company. To be clear, Mateschitz's ask was steep. On paper, he was asking Kastner to brand a subpar-tasting drink that nobody knew about or even knew they needed.[68] But, in Mateschitz's mind, he was asking Kast-

---

[68] David Brown, "Red Bull vs Monster—Get Your Wings," November 13, 2018, in *Business Wars*, produced by Wondery, podcast, 7:13.

ner to brand his dream, a venture he put his entire life savings into and knew instinctively was going to be the next big thing.

"There exists no market for Red Bull," he said at the time, "but we will create one."[69]

They did a modern barter transaction, as Mateschitz was broke at the time after putting all his money into this venture. Mateschitz would freelance consult for Kastner, while Kastner would come up with the packaging and slogan. Over the course of a year and a half, Mateschitz rejected idea after idea, proposal after proposal. Mateschitz was going for perfection and was unwilling to put out the product before it was ready. His patience and dedication were going to pay off in more ways than one.

First, they decided on a logo. Kastner put a spin on Krating Daeng's original logo, two red bulls charging at each other in front of a yellow sun, but he put it on a silver and blue can. The bull is the perfect representation of what Red Bull was supposed to be known for: vitality, strength, life. In nature, we think of the bull as a powerful force, indomitable. That symbolism has crept over to everyday life too. When economies are booming and the stock market is going up, what do we call that? A bull market. This was the perfect symbol for Mateschitz's new energy drink. Not to mention, Red Bull is the literal translation of "Krating Daeng."

Second, they decided on a slogan . . . but not without struggle. In fact, after so many rejected proposals for a slogan, Kastner

---

69   Byrnes, "Dietrich Mateschitz: Raging Bull."

finally told Mateschitz to find another ad agency. Mateschitz asked for one more night. And, as life would have it, that's all they needed. At 3 a.m., Kastner came up with one last idea, "Red Bull Gives You Wings."[70]

WINGS BUT NO FLYING

During that year and a half, however, branding wasn't the only problem Mateschitz was dealing with. Originally, Red Bull was supposed to launch in Germany, but German health officials were alarmed by this new drink. Specifically, they were concerned about what such high amounts of taurine would do to the body. Taurine is an amino acid that is used to facilitate metabolic processes in the body. Today, studies have been conducted that show taurine does have certain healthy benefits like improved human endurance and sports performance.[71] However, back in the 1980s, this knowledge was scarce and German health officials wanted to ensure that the high concentration of taurine was safe.

Mateschitz was dejected but not willing to give up. He decided to move the launch to Austria but was met with obstacles there as well. Austrian officials also wanted testimony from food scientists, chemists, lawyers, and others, to know that the drink was safe to sell. Mateschitz jumped through these hoops and finally won approval from Austrian health officials in 1987.

---

70 David Brown, "Red Bull vs Monster," 10:31.
71 Mawer, "What Is Taurine?"

There was one last thing to do before they launched this exciting new drink: a taste test. He brought together a number of Austrians to sit down, taste Red Bull, and give their honest feedback. Rest assured, they were honest. The drink really didn't taste good. It was really sweet and contained unfamiliar flavors to Europeans. When the tasters were told that Red Bull would also sell at a premium price, one "middle-aged woman wearing red-framed glasses speaks up, 'Is that a joke? That's ridiculous, it's robbery. I wouldn't drink it again if you paid me.'" This taste test was, by all standards, a failure. The man who ran the taste test even recommended that Mateschitz stop there before wasting more time, money, and resources. But he was steadfast.[72]

Mateschitz knew that what makes Red Bull special is not the taste, but the function. It's a performance drink that can enhance athletic endurance and mental capabilities. It's supposed to give you magical powers! Who cares what it tastes like?

"It's not just another flavored sugar water differentiated by color or taste or flavor," he said. "It's an efficiency product. I'm talking about improving endurance, concentration, reaction time, speed, vigilance, and emotional status. Taste is of no importance whatsoever."[73]

Mateschitz was determined to get his drink to market. On April 1, 1987, Red Bull cans made their way to Austria.

---

72 David Brown, "Red Bull vs Monster", 12:49.
73 McDonald, "Red Bull's Billionaire."

WHAT MADE RED BULL FLY OFF THE SHELVES?

Dietrich Mateschitz turned a Thai tonic into a global empire. Red Bull was the first energy drink to enter the global mainstream, so it had no competition. In fact, in the beginning, Coke and Pepsi didn't recognize the non-soda soft drink as a competitor to their beverage brands. By the time they realized this was a serious competitor, they were behind the eight ball in the energy drink sector. Pepsi's Kickstart only hit markets in 2013 and Coca Cola Energy didn't hit US markets until 2020. Red Bull started this $9.5 billion industry and continues to dominate it to this day, owning 38.7 percent of the total industry as of 2019.[74]

Mateschitz succeeded in doing all of this by being meticulous about branding. According to Robert Jones, strategist at brand consultancy firm Wolff Olins and author of *Branding: A Short Introduction,* defines brand as "primarily the 'ideas and feelings a commercial, organizational or cultural entity stands for in people's minds,'" and branding as the "set of things a brand owner does to establish a brand."[75]

It all comes down to two questions: What do you stand for? How do you show people you stand for it?

Red Bull branded itself as an energy drink very deliberately. There's no reason to put your product in the cross hairs of Coca-Cola and Pepsi, two of the largest beverage conglomerates in the world, if you don't have to. Dietrich Mateschitz

---

[74] Claire O'Connor, "US Specialized Industry Report OD4205: Energy Drink Production," accessed August 30, 2020, IBISWorld.

[75] Robert Jones, *Branding: A Very Short Introduction* (Oxford: Oxford University Press, 2017), 15-26.

didn't. He carved out his own niche "energy drink" category to differentiate his product from other soft drinks. Everything Red Bull has done since has been to continue to differentiate, by leaning into this idea of a drink that *does* instead of a drink that just *tastes*.

First came the logo and slogan of "Red Bull," which invokes feelings of vitality and liveliness. This is clearly what you want associated with an energy drink. The red and yellow logo of a bull reinforces this idea as well. But this should be obvious. The much more interesting decisions are more subtle.

Second, when you picture a Red Bull, the immediate thought is the slim blue and silver aluminum can. It is noticeably smaller than a normal soda can, 8.4 fl. oz vs. 12 fl. oz. It's also taller and thinner. It's unique and makes sure that even if you were closing your eyes and you reached out to hold a can, you'd know exactly what you were holding. You can't say the same about Coke or Pepsi.

Third, they adopted a premium image by setting prices "four times more per ounce than average soft drink producers ($1.99–$3.00 per 250 ml can)."[76] This isn't supposed to be a sugary soda; it's an energy supplement, a quality product. The Chinese have a saying called, "一分钱，一分货." Translated in English, it means "You get what you pay for." Having a premium price tells customers that your product is not only different from your competitors, it is better.

---

[76] Paul Farris et al., *Red Bull in Brief* (Charlottesville, VA: University of Virginia—Darden School of Business, 2016).

Lastly, and most importantly, Red Bull pursued a niche multi-pronged marketing strategy based on selling a way of life rather than selling a product by using brand evangelists, "consumer educators," and publicity stunts.

Who are brand evangelists? The customers who love your product so much they market it for you. This is how Red Bull cultivated their own army of brand evangelists. Remember, this is a beverage company trying to carve a new space for itself in the saturated beverage segment, so they became the anti-establishment force in the beverage industry. They didn't want to pursue traditional marketing using TV or banner ads. Rather, they poured their resources into guerrilla marketing. They gave their product away for free to clubs, bars, and dorm rooms in the beginning.[77] They were tapping into the best marketers, their customers themselves. Who do you trust more for a recommendation, an ad on the TV or your friend's word that he was wired for three hours after drinking Red Bull?

In Europe, Red Bull would provide their student representatives with free cases to host parties. At a college campus, one person gets hooked on an energy booster that helped them after a night of partying or kept them awake the night before an exam and ends up telling his closest friends. His friends get hooked and tell their friends. And on and on, until Red Bull cultivates a whole population of students who can't get enough of this stuff.

---

77 Anni L. Rodgers, "It's a (Red) Bull Market after All," *Fast Company*, accessed August 30, 2020.

Red Bull followed this marketing strategy with another ingenious ploy based on Mateschitz's own first experience. Red Bull paid "consumer educators" to drive around in the "Wing Team Car." Hundreds of Mini Coopers were converted into mini-pickup trucks with a sunroof, a super-sized Red Bull Can strapped to the back and painted blue and silver with the Red Bull logo.[78]

Consumer educators would drive around offering tired people a free can of Red Bull. One drive at a time, consumers were experiencing the same magic Dietrich Mateschitz was enchanted by on that fateful trip to Thailand.

What better way to convey "Red Bull gives you wings" than to sponsor people who look like they literally have wings? Red Bull is a specially formulated performance drink meant to wire drinkers with energy and support athletic performance. There is no better way to embody your brand than to pursue a marketing strategy that puts your money where your mouth is. It makes it authentic and compels your customers to believe in your messaging. Red Bull did exactly that and started sponsoring extreme sports from the very first year they were in business. In fact, in 1989, before Red Bull was even founded, Mateschitz had already signed his first celebrity athlete brand ambassador, Austrian Formula 1 driver Gerhard Berger.[79] Now you can see Red Bull at nearly every extreme sporting event from snowboarding to mountain

---

78 Tom Appel, "What Was The Red Bull Car?," *The Daily Drive*, accessed August 30, 2020.

79 Gerhard Berger, "Brief Encounter: The Story of Gerhard Berger and Red Bull," *The Red Bulletin*, March 7, 2020.

biking to cliff jumping.[80] All of these partnerships are tailored to enhance Red Bull's image as the drink of choice for athletes and those who dare. It's exciting, it draws eyeballs, and it's exactly what Mateschitz was going for.

"We would make the brand interesting enough that people wanted to get their hands on it," is how Mateschitz described his marketing strategy.[81] And, in the early years of Red Bull, I'm hard pressed to think of another brand as interesting as Red Bull's. So, if we are talking about brand identity and differentiation, entrepreneurs can take a page out of Mateschitz's book and look for creative ways to connect with customers and drive home the idea that your product is one of a kind. Don't limit your differentiation strategy to just your product; sometimes differentiation through marketing can work wonders as well.

Red Bull is now a leader in content marketing and still avoids traditional marketing. It seems to be working for them. They've sold 6.8 billion cans since 1989 and it doesn't look like they are stopping anytime soon.[82]

---

80   Kaleigh Moore, "Red Bull's Approach to Marketing: Then and Now," *Banknotes*, accessed August 30, 2020.
81   McDonald, "Red Bull's Billionaire."
82   O'Connor, "Industry Report."

CHAPTER 4

VINTNER'S DAUGHTER

―

"Do not try to do everything. Do one thing well."

STEVE JOBS

They said it couldn't be done. She didn't know any better, so she asked, "Why not?" Sometimes, the status quo remains the status quo because no one thought to try something new. What's the saying? "Why fix something that's not broken?" The thing is something is broken. We just don't know it yet. But April Gargiulo cracked the code after one fateful trip to Morocco. This is the story of Vintner's Daughter. She brought together the ideals of fine wine making to commercialized skin care and, in the process, revolutionized the industry. Let's start from the beginning.

April Gargiulo didn't come from the land of cosmetics and beauty. She came from the world of grape vines and oak barrels. Her family owns and operates Gargiulo Vineyards, a Napa Valley vineyard and estate-producing Cabernet

Sauvignon.[83] She grew up with an appreciation for quality ingredients, meticulous processes, and the knowledge that it can take a long time to create something great.

Throughout her life, she had struggled with her skin, whether it was cystic acne when she was young or discoloration with her skin as she got older. Her philosophy at the time was to try everything. If this skin care product doesn't work, the next one is bound to. For many people, this is a very real and very common reality. We will try this cream and that serum as long as we think there is a chance for it to be the holy grail that clears up the face. Gargiulo was no different. If it was sold on a shelf, she had probably used it before. However, nothing quite worked the way she wanted it to.

YOU NEVER KNOW WHAT YOU MIGHT DISCOVER.
Then, she went to Morocco with her husband on vacation. For most people, the hotel, a bar, or the beach is the first place they would want to go when they touch down at their destination. But not Gargiulo; she booked it straight to an apothecary or pharmacy to find a new product to save her skin with the same conviction as someone trying to find the elixir of life.

For most of us, "apothecary" conjures up an image of a dark lair with pots bubbling and an aura of mysticism. I'm going to take the mystery out of it. An apothecary a couple hundred years ago might've looked like something Severus Snape

---

83 Joanna Czech, "April Gargiulo," *Joanna Czech*, accessed September 14, 2020.

would be proud to see, but an apothecary now is a version of a modern pharmacy selling herbal and other natural remedies. But I digress. When April touched down in Morocco, she found herself in this hundred-year-old apothecary with dirt floors and shelves upon shelves of hand-marked glass jars filled with herbs, powders, salts, spices, and more. Each jar had something different and there were hundreds of jars.

The woman at the apothecary didn't speak English and April didn't speak Arabic, so there was no way for her to tell this woman what she was looking for. Luckily April didn't have to, but she didn't know that in the beginning. This woman took one look at April's face and pointed to an oil.

Of all the things that oils are known to be used for, treating the face with them is not the most common thought. Truly, it's kind of counterintuitive; most people don't want to look oily, so why would they voluntarily put oil on their face?

This is the kind of internal dialogue I would be having if I were April standing in front of this woman. So, in a kind of pantomime sequence that probably would have made good black and white comedy, this woman points to an oil and April points to her face. The woman, again, points to this oil. April, again, points to her face and says, "No, no, no, no. You don't understand."[84] But, this woman was adamant, and like I said, April had tried *everything*.

---

[84] Danielle Snyder, "Minimal Skincare, Maximum Impact | No Filter Ep. 11 Vintner's Daughter," October 29, 2019, in *No Filter with Danielle Snyder*, produced by Danielle Snyder, podcast, 7:20.

Later that night, she went back to her hotel room and thought to herself, "I'm jumping off a cliff. I'm about to put oil on my skin. What, have I lost my mind?"[85]

She woke up the next morning with her skin feeling more balanced and clearer than it had been in a very long time. This was a game-changing moment for her. Speaking about this moment in an interview, April says, "This is what I had been doing wrong. I've been fighting with my skin all this time. And, every time I'm trying to strip it of this oil, my skin knows what to do: it's producing more because it wants to balance."[86] Now, armed with this new knowledge of how oils could benefit her skin, she was on the perfect path to take care of her skin. Fifteen years after that chance experience in Morocco, she started Vintner's Daughter and their first product: Active Botanical Serum.

But, there's more to the story.

WINEMAKING X SKIN CARE
When April was pregnant with her first child, she started reading the labels of all the products she was putting into her body, including skin care. Like, seriously reading the label. And, she didn't like what she saw. In the luxury skin care products she was using, the content often looked something like this: 0.01 percent active ingredient, filler, filler, and more filler. For April, this was unacceptable. She's not just a consumer who wanted to be getting more money's worth than

---

85 Snyder, "Minimal Skincare," 7:36.
86 Snyder, "Minimal Skincare," 8:02.

a fraction of a fraction of the good stuff and 99.99 percent of the whatever; April is also part of the wine world. A world where every single grape is analyzed and every grain of dirt is judged for quality. A world where luxury means, "starting with the finest ingredients, and honoring those ingredients from very meticulous, very quality-focused formulation practices."[87] A world that didn't just settle for 0.01 percent of an active ingredient like the skin care industry commonly does. In the wine world, they only settle for 100 percent of the active ingredient.

So, what does an entrepreneur with a winemaking background do to a multibillion-dollar industry that just wasn't really cutting it? She started a "skin care company and a skin care product that was built on the same philosophical foundations as fine winemaking, of quality and craftsmanship and ultimately performance."[88] She wanted to offer the market something it didn't really have anymore, a skin care product in which every ingredient had a purpose. She knew her product would change people's skin for the better; but there was no way for her to know that her product, Active Botanical Serum, would also change the game of modern cosmetics.

ACTIVE BOTANICAL SERUM

April embarked on a two-year journey full of obstacles and unintended surprises. Thinking back to that life-changing experience with oil in Morocco and paying homage to her

---

87 Kirbie Johnson and Sara Tan, "How Wine Inspired a Cult-Favorite Serum with April Gargiulo from Vintner's Daughter," November 12, 2019, in *Gloss Angeles*, produced by Kirbie Johnson, podcast, 23:00.

88 Johnson and Tan, "How Wine Inspired," 23:10.

winemaking roots, April started with grapeseed oil as a base. She thought, "If I am going to be using oil as my base, how do I use oil as my trojan horse? How do I fill it with as much nutrients as I can, and as much performance driven ingredients that I can?"[89]

Here's why grapeseed oil made for the perfect base. First, grapeseed oil is full of antioxidants and omega-3s, which have a myriad of health benefits to the skin by themselves. Second, it has a small particle size, which allows it to act as an ideal carrier for other oils. Third, she comes from the wine world, so she knows where to get the highest quality grapeseed oil.[90]

From grapeseed oil, the rest of the ingredients fell into place, one led right to the other. She then added cypress leaf oil, which reduces redness and calms irritation.[91] But its effects are magnified when used in conjunction with frankincense, which increases circulation of blood under the skin. One by one, these natural ingredients were infused in the highest concentrations until April and her team came up with twenty-two of the world's finest and most active botanicals to create the powerful Active Botanical Serum.

"I really believe that just like in food, there are certain things that make other things vibrate at a higher frequency or work better on your skin. So, we have a real deep respect for that.

---

89 Snyder, "Minimal Skincare," 8:28.

90 "Active Botanical Serum," Vintner's Daughter, accessed August 9, 2020.

91 Victoria Lewis, "The Face Oil to End All Face Oils," *Into the Gloss*, accessed September 14, 2020.

Every ingredient we use is because mixed together they work better," April said.[92] Each whole plant is infused into the oil at the highest concentration allowed at the most optimal ratios. April was not messing around when she said she wanted her product to be 100 percent performative and made with the best ingredients she could find.

In fact, she was so adamant about honoring this process and these botanicals that she went around the world to source each of the twenty-two ingredients. She gets her ingredients "from the best, most conscious farmers around the world. There are some things that just grow better in certain places. Our hazelnut oil comes from a farm in the Piedmont region in Italy. They've been growing and producing this hazelnut oil for generations. Our Cyprus is wild crafted from the coast of Spain, our tomato oil comes from a co-op of growers in Madagascar, our rose oil comes from a family that's been growing and producing the most amazing organic rose oil from Bulgaria, and our neroli oil comes from Morocco."[93]

April extrapolated the very best qualities of winemaking, which is paying attention to where things come from and not just the things themselves, because often, if you can find the best environment, you'll get the best product. This kind of care isn't commonly seen in the cosmetic industry.

In fact, April flew against the grain of nearly every single thing that the cosmetic industry is predicated on. Most skin

---

92 Gillian Sagansky, "How a Former Winemaker Ended Up Making Gwyneth Paltrow's Go-To Serum," *W Magazine*, accessed August 9, 2020.

93 Ibid.

care products have very few active ingredients, are made in a lab with certain cost-saving formulations, and only take a few hours to make. However, when April was searching for labs to produce Active Botanical Serum and told them what she was expecting, they thought she was crazy, and many rejected her. *This just wasn't how things were done.*

"Remember, I was coming from Napa Valley where it takes three years to make a bottle of wine, so for me, I thought, 'We are going to make the best skin care in the world and it's *only* going to take three weeks.'"[94] April's dedication to using the best ingredients and not rushing the process is what makes Active Botanical Serum a cult favorite and cosmetic game changer.

This **one** product is made to be so powerful and so healing that you don't have to use anything else on your face. Dubbed *the face oil to end all face oils* by Victoria Lewis from Into the Gloss, Active Botanical Serum is the perfect mixture of twenty-two ingredients, but it's also the perfect mixture of nature's gift to human beings, a winemaking ethos, and one trip to Morocco.

IF YOU TAKE CARE OF YOUR PRODUCTS, THEY CAN TAKE CARE OF YOU.
Vintner's Daughter is not known for having a diverse range of products to choose from, and this is a conscious decision not many others in the industry make. But April's decision to make Vintner's Daughter a monobrand and stay that way

---

94   Johnson and Tan, "How Wine Inspired," 24:30.

for many years has been a clear differentiator from its competitors, and also the reason for its success.

So, what exactly is a monobrand? Simply put, it is a single product company; you can think notebook company Moleskin, clog-flip-flop company Crocs, or luxury coat company Moncler. In fact, many major conglomerates and industry powerhouses started off with just *one product* before deciding to expand years later, like Coke for Coca-Cola, ties for Ralph Lauren, and sheepskin boots for Ugg Australia.

These companies are all testaments that one idea can be enough. Here's why:

WHEN YOU ONLY HAVE ONE PRODUCT, YOU CAN POUR ALL ATTENTION INTO MAINTAINING YOUR BRAND IMAGE.

The beauty of only having one product means you don't have to split your time focusing on other products that might not serve your brand. You can pour one hundred percent of your time and resources into perfecting the one product you are bringing to the market and to your consumers. Vintner's Daughter is the perfect example for this. Gargiulo wouldn't compromise on time, ingredients, or other products when she was originally formulating Active Botanical Serum. This led to a number of manufacturers refusing to make the serum simply because they felt they could get better profit margins manufacturing multiple products that use cheaper ingredients and take a fraction of the time to make. This also led to some retailers not picking up the product.

"No one took us seriously. Retailers didn't pick us up because they didn't know where to put us on a shelf. They would fall in love with Active Botanical Serum and then they'd say, 'Just call me back when you've got another product.' And I would say, 'Well, I might not have another product.'"[95]

But Gargiulo stuck to her guns and "remained disciplined [on] our commitment to produce only **game changing, category defining products.**"[96] When your process is as complex as extracting the nutrients of twenty-two different ingredients sourced from all over the world and then infusing them to be as active and powerful as possible, it deserves all twenty-one days to completion.

Her philosophy for Vintner's Daughter is this: "We only make products that are going to transform your skin. And for us that is a constraint, but it's a constraint that we joyfully and gratefully embrace."[97] She isn't looking to create a hundred individual products for her customers to use in conjunction. Rather, she is focused on creating one product so masterful that it is the only one you would need. Monobrand isn't a marketing ploy for Vintner's Daughter; it's their foundation of success.

---

95 Johnson and Tan, "How Wine Inspired," 25:29.
96 Snyder, "Minimal Skincare," 21:31.
97 Snyder, "Minimal Skincare," 21:49.

WHEN YOU ONLY HAVE ONE PRODUCT, YOU CAN TRULY FOCUS ON MAKING IT BETTER.

Growing up, my parents always said to me, "Don't just work hard, work smart. Don't do a million things and stretch yourself thin. Do one thing and then go on to the other one." They were right and the science backs it up too.

In 2012, Amy Dalton and Stephen Spiller, professor from the Hong Kong University of Science and Technology and assistant professor from Anderson School of Management at UCLA respectively, conducted an experiment on people's exercise habits based on factors like implementation intention and number of goals. What they found is that "the benefits of implementation intentions for a single goal do not extend to multiple goals... by compromising commitment at the planning stage, forming implementation intentions compromises success at the execution stage."[98] Ultimately, when you spread yourself too thin by trying to accomplish too many things, you end up not doing great on any of the things. You are much better suited focusing the planning on one thing completely to ensure successful execution.

Bringing a product or service to market is an endeavor that takes serious and meticulous planning. When planning for one thing, you can pour all focus and attention to solving that problem or creating that product. Active Botanical Serum wasn't created in the blink of an eye; it went through stages of making things better and better until there was nothing left to add. But by practicing and doing the steps over and

---

98   Amy N. Dalton and Stephen A. Spiller, "Too Much of a Good Thing: The Benefits of Implementation Intentions Depend on the Number of Goals," *Journal of Consumer Research* 39, no. 3 (2012): 600-614.

over, it is easier to cut out inefficiencies and find better ways to infuse, extract, or package. If Gargiulo had to worry about this arduous process for a line of products, there just simply wouldn't have been enough time in the day to do everything necessary to create such a high-quality product across the board. By focusing on one Active Botanical Serum, she was able to create something so positively potent, nothing else in the market comes close. This is not only a differentiator to competitors, but a value proposition that enhances the company brand as well.

WHEN YOU ONLY HAVE ONE PRODUCT, THERE IS NO SHORTAGE OF WAYS TO EXPAND.

I believe that when you do one product well, you create a reputation for your brand and build lasting relationships with your customers. People cannot get enough of a great thing, especially for a product in the skin care industry. Everyone in the world cares about having great skin because it can be a source of confidence. This means that if you can create a product that resonates, you can keep those customers forever. A serum is not a one-time purchase; it's a purchase that customers will make time and time again. And this is what April taps into with Active Botanical Serum and her niche of customers: "We want to create a heritage skin care company that you use, your mother uses, your daughter uses, that because we are creating products that are timeless that will always service the skin."[99]

---

99 Johnson and Tan, "How Wine Inspired," 41:46.

The added benefit of having such captive and engaged customers is they will tell you exactly what they want next. As a monobrand with such high-quality products, Vintner's Daughter is not lacking in inspiration for the next product. "We have incredible customers, and they have incredible ideas. We asked people on Instagram the other day and [their] answer was body, SPF, cleanser, and a cream. This is what everybody wanted," comments Gargiulo when prompted about what could be next.[100] This is an incredible advantage for an entrepreneur because they will never have to worry that their product won't be in demand.

Another testimonial comes from the Masterclass of Sara Blakely, CEO of Spanx, another monobrand company, who said, "I spent about seven to eight hours a day for two years straight in department stores, listening to customers, getting my next best ideas. I had no other inventions up my sleeve. But they all gave me my next best ideas."[101] Simply put, there is already demand for a product you haven't even formulated yet and the people who would buy it are the people telling you to make it. This puts you at a business advantage best pictured like this: A million competitive runners are at the starting line of a marathon, and you get to start one mile ahead of everyone else. Who doesn't want to start a mile in?

In so intensively pursuing an active skin care product, April Gargiulo utilized the patience and attention to detail of a winemaker and shook up the whole skin care industry. After

---

100 Johnson and Tan, "How Wine Inspired," 40:05.
101 Sara Blakely, "Build Awareness," accessed September 20, 2020, in *Sara Blakely Teaches Self-Made Entrepreneurship*, produced by Masterclass, video, 13:41.

being inspired by a mysterious Moroccan oil, she came up with Active Botanical Serum and stuck with it for five years before coming out with her second product, Active Treatment Essence. Aided by the benefits of a monobrand, she created award winning next-level quality skin care products that will continue to serve her customers' skin care needs for generations. Entrepreneurs can take this as a blueprint to create their own category-defining products in their respective industries, be it tech, fashion, cleaning product, and anything else. And the one thing not in the blueprint? An expectation that you need to start off with or even end up with multiple ideas. Sometimes, one can be enough.

CHAPTER 5

PAYJOY

———

"It's almost always harder to raise capital than you thought it would be, and it always takes longer. So plan for that."
RICHARD HARROCH.[102]

THE TWO CRUCIAL THINGS OF THE 21ST CENTURY: CREDIT AND SMARTPHONES

If you don't have it, borrow it. What are we talking about? Loans. Debt. Credit. The foundation of capitalism. This is not an economics lesson, but it is important to point out that banking and financial institutions have proliferated people's access to money. And let's not be coy about it; it's the backbone of modern economies. Person A loans Person B $100. Person B spends the money on something that gains in value to get a return of 20 percent, so that original $100 turns into $120. The pie just got bigger. Our modern-day financial institutions do this transaction all day long, seven days a week,

---

[102] Sujan Patel, "21 Success Tips for Young and Aspiring Entrepreneurs," *Entrepreneur*, accessed February 8, 2021.

in quantities that are each orders of magnitudes larger than the last. Everyone is supposed to get richer.

Credit has offered thousands of millions of people paths to financial success and even wealth. How do people pay for things that they want, like a bigger house or a fancier car when they don't have the money for it? They take out a loan or get a mortgage. If they get lucky and the economy is in the right spot, the bank just might offer single-digit interest rates.

But how do people with no access to a bank get the money to pay for things they need? Well, the most common answer is that they either have the money or they don't. The less common answer is that the *few* people who have access to credit get it from loan sharks who charge a 500 percent interest rate. The issue with the latter is obvious, but there is an even bigger problem.

If you have never borrowed money before, you have no credit. No credit means no credit history. No credit history means you can't get an approved loan for things that might actually earn you money if you ever do get access to a bank. It's like the negative circle of money with no way in, no way out, and just frustration for everyone involved. *It can be equated to college students' frustrations about getting their first job. Obviously, they've never worked before, but no company will hire someone without prior experience. It's the gift that keeps on giving.*

Now, if you think access to money is the big problem these days, let me ask, what about access to smartphones?

It is hard for many of us to picture our lives without our phones. No, I'm sorry, let me be more specific. It's hard for many of us to picture our lives without our *smartphones*. It is not only a device for us to call our loved ones; it is now also a high definition camera, photo album of our lives, module for conference calls, extension of our work desktop, handheld doctor, calorie tracker, music player, podcast player, GPS tracker for our other devices, GPS for the road, game console, streaming device, diary, pocket weatherman, digital car key, home security system, and digital bank. It is the window into the twenty-first century. It is the window into the online world. It is the window into our lives. I really could go on and on. But I digress. Now, I want you to think about your life without your smartphone.

How do you communicate? How do you get anywhere? How do you buy anything?

This might sound like an exaggeration, but I really don't think I'm too far off. I can't imagine how I would go about my life without my smartphone and I'm willing to bet the 3.5 billion smartphone users all over the world would agree with me.[103] Did you catch it? The problem in the last sentence? That many smartphone users sound like a lot until it is put into the context of the whole world. That is only 44.85 percent of the global population. Less than half the people in the world own a smartphone, something that those who have it arguably can't live without. What about the other 55.15 percent who don't have it because they don't have the money to pay for it?

---

103 Ash Turner, "How Many Smartphones Are in the World?" *BankMyCell* (blog), *BankMyCell*, accessed September 19, 2020.

PayJoy founders Doug Ricket, Mark Heynen, and Gib Lopez set out to solve this very real, and very current, problem. But the path to their solution goes *way* back.

LET'S START WITH DOUG RICKET.
Ricket is a serial entrepreneur. For his master's project at MIT, he founded MIT's Women's Technology Program, which was a summer school program dedicated to helping female students learn engineering at MIT. They have since graduated over 500 students in the last fifteen years. But after a year, Ricket moved on to public service and moved to West Africa to do it. Joining the Peace Corps, he taught programming to students at the University of Gambia while also volunteering at Gambia's National Electric Company.

Here, he realized their electric system wasn't working like a well-oiled machine. Under that original system, customers would use electricity for one month and pay whatever it cost in one lump sum at the end of the month. This is the way most people around the world do it. However, the difference in Gambia is that when people don't pay their electricity bill, the electric company comes to the house to take the electric meter out. It is only reinstalled after the customer has paid the fine. It's a highly inefficient system where many customers weren't paying their electricity bills in full, and in turn the company doesn't always get paid.

After Gambia, Ricket took a four-year stint working on Google Maps and met Mark Heynen. *Pin this thought, we'll get back to it in a bit.* During this four-year period, back in Gambia, the electric company flipped the utilities system on its head. When he returned, he saw something he had never seen before. The electric company was using a whole new system to avoid missed payments. They were using a technologically advanced electric system that allowed customers to avoid accumulating a large electricity bill to be paid at the end of the month, and instead allowed them to pay for their usage at a kiosk before they used it. Pay what you want and don't worry about overspending.

"So, you go to the corner shop, you pay ten dollars, enter the code and now you've got fifty kilowatt hours of electricity. The meter counts down to zero, and then the lights shut off," is how Ricket describes it.[104] Now the company doesn't have to worry about uncollectible accounts receivables and additional expenses to pay an employee to uninstall and later reinstall the electric meter. To top it off, the customer doesn't have to worry about their electricity over-usage and fines. It was a perfect solution.

D.LIGHT DESIGN TO LIGHT THE WAY

Ricket, inspired by what he saw in Gambia, took this very idea and incorporated it into a new venture—D.light Design—after leaving Google. D.light Design is a startup selling solar lighting kits in India and Africa.[105] Many people in these countries were burning kerosene for lighting and cooking. *Kerosene is the same thing we put in jet engines.* People were using jet fuel for daily use and breathing in the fumes, which

---

[104] James R. Koren, "Got No Credit? Payjoy Will Finance Your Phone—but Turn It into a Brick If You Don't Pay," *Hartford Courant*, December 2, 2016.

[105] "Doug Ricket," *TechTycoons*, accessed August 6.

caused lung problems and a myriad of other health issues. D.light Design was offering a safer and more sustainable alternative. They were offering a bundle of solar panels, bulbs, battery indicators, and wall switches for $200 in total.

But they were running into the same problem the electric company was before. The $200 was more than what many people and families could afford, and, with no access to credit, there was no way for customers to access this superior alternative to kerosene. Ricket figured out a way to mimic the electric company's strategy by inserting a financial technology system that can remotely disable the product. Customers would prepay usage of the solar panels and D.light would automatically shut off the power when the credit ran to zero. D.light Design was able to adopt the pay-as-you-need approach that made the whole business transaction more economically feasible for everyone involved. Doug Ricket patented this technology before he went back to attend Stanford Graduate School of Business.

Here is where we dial the story back to Mark Heynen. After Ricket left for West Africa in 2009, Heynen left for Facebook one year later. He was responsible for the penetration strategy of Facebook in emerging markets. The value of joining Facebook is obvious: More than one billion people use it. It's one of the best apps to connect with others online, in addition to the myriad of other services Facebook provides. But the key word is "online." To get onto Facebook's platform you need a device that has the capability to download the app and connect to internet capabilities. Low-end phones don't have the capabilities and developers know there is no money here to develop the software to make that possible. Why expend limited resources to create something that only a very small population of people who are financially challenged can buy? Unfortunately, the terrible reality is that there's no real profit to be made here. It's the same problem pharmaceutical companies have. Why create a drug only a handful of people need with no path to profits?

But Heynen knew the circumstances with the smartphone market were different. With no cheaper options, customers have no choice but to turn to higher end, expensive smartphones that have up-to-standard connectivity. And it isn't just a handful of people who need a smartphone but can't afford it; it's nearly two billion people. Mark Heynen believed, "The next two billion people aren't going to have credit, and the $100 functional smartphone doesn't exist yet. For the next two billion people, the smartphone is going to be their first computer."[106]

Doug Ricket wanted to change that. He met Gib Lopez, who was another MBA student at Stanford Graduate School of Business and had personal experience seeing the need for development in places like Mexico where his extended family lives. Together, they got Mark Heynen on board to start PayJoy in August of 2015.

---

106 Jonathan Shieber, "With $4.3 Million Payjoy Is Ensuring Smartphones Land in the Hands of the Next 2 Billion," *Tech Crunch*, December 18, 2015.

PAYJOY: CREDIT AND SMARTPHONE ACCESS FOR THOSE WHO NEED IT MOST

The three entrepreneurs wanted to revolutionize the smartphone industry in emerging markets all over the world and in their backyard. Working with a number of partners like Telefonica, MetroPCS, and Boost, they started rolling out their pay-as-you-go smartphone service in Mexico and have expanded to a number of countries in South America and Africa as well as four states in the United States. Their customers just need a government-issued form of identification, a Facebook account (for verification purposes), and a phone number, and PayJoy will front 80 percent of the cost and install their software into the smartphone. Over the next three to twelve months, customers will pay fixed installments of up to 50 percent more than the original cost.

While this may seem large, it is just a fraction of what loan sharks would require for a loan like this. Before PayJoy, there just weren't that many options for financing without a credit score.

Gib Lopez had this to say about the topic: "Lending for smartphone purchase tends to only be available to the top 5 to 10 percent of the population. People that already have plenty of money, documented income, credit history are the ones that the system already works for."[107] And for the other 90 to 95 percent of people, they used to be subject to predatory lending which charges interest rates more than double what PayJoy offers.

---

107 Jumoke Akiyode-Lawanson, "Our Goal Is to Deliver Access to Smartphone Financing Technology," *Business Day*, November 12, 2019.

So how does this all work? The same way the solar lighting kits do. Every month, users would pay their portion for the month. If there is a missed payment, the phone automatically locks with only two viable dials, 911 for emergency services and the PayJoy service line, until the user puts more money in. And, at any point in time, the customer can give the phone back at no extra cost.[108]

While we still have a long way to go to really achieve full scale accessibility to smartphones for every person on Earth, this is a good, solid leap. Their customers not only gain access to the resources they need, but PayJoy's service also offers an added benefit. For many, this will be their first loan, their first line of credit to build their credit history.

PayJoy is welcoming their users to the modern financial system and the modern technological system. These opportunities have been long overdue. PayJoy is just one example of many businesses that are meshing serious profitability with social good.

"When we think about shifts in technology and the economy, it has become clear that the smartphone will be at the epicenter of work and education for the next decade," said David Hirsch, Metamorphic Ventures founder and managing director who was part of the initial $2.3 million funding round. "However, there's still a huge barrier to entry in buying a smartphone for much of the population. PayJoy's unique

---

108 Koren, "Got No Credit?"

software-enabled financing solution completely erases this barrier and can significantly improve people's lives."[109]

It's not God's work, but it is necessary. And, they wouldn't have gotten the idea without initial trips to Gambia, India, and Mexico. People often say modern problems need modern solutions. I say emerging market problems need emerging market solutions.

IT'S ALL ABOUT THE MONEY.
Great ideas are everywhere, but money is not. What separates the great ideas that stay as ideas and the great ideas that turn into unicorn companies are entrepreneurs who decided to go for it *and* had the money to fund the venture in the first place. No matter what kind of product or service you are trying to put out into the world, capital is just a necessary component to your success. Without it, it's just hard to get off the ground.

One of the first things an entrepreneur has to do is raise money. Victoria Tsai did it by selling her engagement ring and car. David Chang, founder of Momofuku, and Gordon and Carole Segal, founders of Crate & Barrel, did it by getting seed money from their fathers. Howard Schultz did it by convincing venture capitalists to fund his dream.

In Schultz's MasterClass episode titled *Find the Right Investors*, he begins by saying, "Raising money is always hard."[110]

---

109 Shieber, "With $4.3 Million."
110 Howard Schultz, "Find the Right Investors," accessed October 13, 2020, in *Howard Schultz Business Leadership*, Produced by MasterClass, video, 0:13.

This makes sense. There are a lot of questions and things to consider. How much money does this venture need? What is the best funding path? Where does the money come from? When is the right time to do it?

Every founder CEO has a decision to make: what to do about funding?

Here are the options:

SELF-FUNDING

Self-fund (also known as bootstrapping): This first type of capital relies on being *lean*. There is no form of outside capital. Some entrepreneurs will choose to fund their venture with their own money, whether it comes from their personal savings account, selling personal assets, and/or funneling all of the income earned from the business back into the business. The key to using this strategy is to truly minimize all costs and rely on being scrappy. This often means doing many things yourself, such as marketing your business through social media or building your own online marketplace.

Depending on your business model, you might have very high up-front costs or next to none if you are offering a service. But no matter what you are selling, at the very least there is an opportunity cost. If you are pursuing your venture, the time that goes into your startup cannot be shared with anything else. By choosing to do this, you can't choose to do anything else.[111] When people say, "time is money," this is what they mean.

The advantages of self-funding is that entrepreneurs can retain full ownership and control of their company. If you put all of the money and time into a project, you own it and all the profits return to you. There is no additional step to pay off any debts or give up any equity, and you really learn how to be an entrepreneur. The beauty of doing everything by yourself is that this is an opportunity to practice selling and marketing your product, which are key skills entrepreneurs need anyway.

The disadvantages of self-funding is that it's hard to scale or expand your business. For my chemistry majors out there, there is a concept called "limiting reagent," which refers to when a chemical reaction needs multiple elements to form one product; the element that gets totally consumed first limits the amount of product that can be created. In this case, money is the limiting reagent. When you run out of money, you can't keep producing. If growth is the priority, having limited funds is, simply put, not ideal. Additionally, if you are looking for mentorship or a network, you lose out on both of these items by choosing self-funding over other types of capital.

Victoria Tsai is a great example of a founder who took advantage of self-funding. By selling her car and engagement ring, she was able to take Tatcha in whatever direction she wanted

---

111 Danielle Sutton, "The Ultimate Introductory Guide to Funding Your Social Enterprise," *Acumen Academy* (blog), *Acumen Academy*, July 27, 2019.

to go. Even when other people, like her suppliers, were telling her to use cheaper products or retailers didn't want to carry blotting papers because it was a standalone product, Victoria was able to shape Tatcha exactly to her vision and nobody else's. Day in and day out, she pitched her business to retailers, suppliers, and customers, and every day she got better at telling her story, Tatcha's story. Eventually, she pitched to everyone else enough that venture capitalists and investors turned around and began pitching to *her* to become a financial backer of Tatcha.

FRIENDS AND FAMILY

Friends and Family: This type of capital comes from exactly where you think it does, from *your* friends and family. Calling up your inner circle to invest in you is not necessarily easier than asking for money from a stranger, but at least you already have a foot in the door. Sometimes it really is easier to convince people who already know you, your work ethic, and your dream to come on this crazy entrepreneurial ride with you. But, at the same time, mixing business and pleasure is tricky. There is more skin in the game because you are using other people's money that more often than not must be paid back. Relationships can be made or broken at this juncture, so it's best to go into this arrangement with eyes wide open. This means having an agreement with all expectations written out regarding repayment and other terms and conditions. If there is ever a time to compartmentalize business and personal, now is it.

The advantages of friends and family capital is that this is likely the cheapest form of capital that you can raise outside of investing your own money. When your friends and family give you money, they truly are investing in you. The focus is less on your business plan, future market headwinds, or lack of a prior track record. There is also an added benefit that your friends and family should be easier to negotiate with than a bank or venture capitalist when trying to change the terms of the agreement down the line.

The disadvantage of friends and family capital is that there is a risk of strained or broken relationships. Money is a taboo issue to talk about already, so mixing investing in a relationship is tricky. There must be transparent and open communication from the very beginning so that no party in this agreement is caught off guard. Whether it means that the entrepreneur is never able to return the money, there is misunderstanding about a repayment, or even the other way around with a friend or family member pulling their funding and leaving the entrepreneur with nothing, there are as many things that can go wrong as there are things that can go right. It is also difficult to raise a lot of capital, so again, if scaling is your goal, this might not be enough.

David Chang, restauranteur and founder of Momofuku restaurant group would know. His original $130,000 to open up a restaurant in Manhattan was not without risk. He was about to enter into one of the most competitive and tough markets in the world with what is truly a very limited number of funds. Remember, he had just enough money to pay for rent, salary, and food to operate the first Momofuku storefront. Decorations and profits only happened way down the line in the future. But in the beginning, Chang was entering an industry with a reputation of ninety percent failure (now debunked, it's closer to sixty percent).[112]

Understandably, he viewed Momofuku as a gamble and was so afraid of losing his father's and his friends' money that he spent three years working nonstop and said this of that period, "I was terrified. I viewed it as life or death."[113] And this sentiment is not special to David. Being responsible for someone else's money is stressful, but being responsible for your friend or family member's money is personal. It's more than just money; it's also your relationship.

CROWDFUNDING

Crowdfunding: A relatively new funding option that became available due to the internet, founders can create an account on sites like Kickstarter.com, indiegogo.com, gofundme.com, and many others. This is truly a democratized way of funding by leaning into the power of the people. It's harder to convince one person to give a large sum of money than to convince many people to give a small sum of money. There are a number of different types of crowdfunding with the most common being a rewards-based system where investors like you and me are able to invest anywhere from five dollars to one hundred dollars in exchange for perks in early releases or product prototypes.

---

112 G. Sidney, "Restaurant Failure Rates Recounted: Where Do They Get Those Numbers?," *RestaurantOwner.com*, accessed October 12, 2020.

113 "How Momofuku's David Chang Turned His Dream into a Global Food Brand," *JPMorgan Chase & Co.*, accessed October 12, 2020.

There are other options that involve investors getting a share of equity or an option for a loan in which investors would receive interest on top of a principal. For all the skeptics out there who couldn't imagine this type of funding being successful (me being one of them in the beginning), crowdfunding has raised millions of dollars from millions of supporters. One example is Tile, the Bluetooth item tracker, which raised $200,000 in funding in the first day and $2.5 million in total.[114]

The advantages of crowdfunding for founders are the social and financial capital you can build. You can think of each supporter who "donates" or "invests" in your start-up idea as a future customer, someone who found enough value in your company to decide they want to give you money. This is a great way to gauge market demand for your service, and especially your product. In fact, for the rewards-based product crowdfunding campaigns, your backers can receive your new product and give you feedback. And a great product doesn't stay a secret often. Because crowdfunding is so accessible, if you can effectively campaign your product and gain supporters, those supporters can market for you by telling their friends too. This is a great way raise venture capital if that is a future goal as this campaign can show any potential investors that your product is legit and demanded by the market.

The disadvantage of crowdfunding is the additional time and effort necessary to run a campaign. It takes time to

---

[114] Emily Heaslip, "9 Wildly Successful Crowdfunded Startups," CO, published October 1, 2019.

successfully crowdfund, get enough people to donate, and raise necessary funds. For rewards-based campaigns, founders have to pay for the perks given to their supporters which means founders have additional expenses to cover. Additionally, there is a time component to campaigns in that there is an expected return in a timely manner as indicated by your campaign, whether in the form of a physical product or interest.

Many companies today have started with a crowdfunded campaign. Oculus, the virtual reality headset that takes gaming and entertainment to the next level, raised $250,000 dollars within four hours on Kickstarter. The founders used that money to develop the software and hardware which eventually was sold to Facebook for two billion dollars in 2014.[115] The movie *Veronica Mars* was even crowdfunded by fans on Kickstarter who helped the director, Rob Thomas, raise one million dollars in the first four hours and two million in the first twelve hours, which was a goal Thomas feared "was a ridiculous amount of money to ask for."[116]

DEBT

Debt: One of the classic and most common ways to obtain money is to take on debt that must be paid back within a certain period of time with additional interest. Debt capital usually comes from a bank in the form of a commercial loan which could be a term loan or revolving line of credit. A term

---

[115] Ibid.
[116] Sarah Rappaport, "Kickstarter Funding Brings 'Veronica Mars' Movie to Life," *CNBC*, March 12, 2014.

loan is your classic loan with a set repayment schedule, and it is usually used for financing the purchase of a big ticket asset like equipment. The founder would be responsible for paying back the full amount of principal with all additional accrued interest. A revolving line of credit can be thought of like a large credit card. The bank or lender would authorize a certain amount in credit that the founder is able to use as needed. The founder will have to repay the debt periodically but would only pay interest on the amount of money used. This type of loan is primarily used for companies affected by seasonal changes or those who have a temporary shortfall in cash and need this bridge loan for operational purposes.

The advantage of debt is primarily that founders will not lose any equity or control. For founders who need a significant investment but don't want to give up any control of the company, this is the way to do it. This is a temporary measure that gives founders the flexibility capital-wise that they need to operate but does not tie them into an agreement indefinitely. A founder can get a bank loan to expand operations and to increase revenues and efficiency. At a certain point, founders would be able to earn enough revenue that after the loan is paid off, they won't need another line of credit and can operate by themselves.

The disadvantage of debt is that it is difficult to get a bank loan. Banks are notoriously risk averse in their investments and unlikely to offer a loan that has too much risk. This means that before you approach a bank, you should have a history of creditworthiness, which involves both you personally, your business, and collateral you can put up. Most lenders will look for multiple levels of repayment in the case of a default, such as marking equipment, the building, land, and any other assets as collateral. If these aren't available, they might ask for a personal guarantee, which places a significant amount of liability on the founder who would be on the hook for the loan in the case that the company goes bankrupt.

Many companies choose this avenue of funding as demonstrated by a healthy and growing commercial banking industry. The original coffee-bean Starbucks with Bowker, Baldwin, and Siegl actually started with a bank loan. They needed the money to pay rent and buy inventory, but they didn't want to give up equity of the company to do it. Each partner put up $1,500 dollars and they successfully secured a $5,000 bank loan to get them started.[117] Another company who got started with a small loan is the British skin care company, The Body Shop. Anita Roddick took out a $5,000 bank loan to purchase ethically sourced, non-animal tested, and natural ingredients to make beauty products sold in a small store in Brighton, UK, that revolutionized the way business can be used for positive social change.[118]

EQUITY

Equity: The standard way to raise money for startups, especially in the tech sector, is through equity capital. Venture capitalists and angel investors will invest an amount of money in your company which doesn't have to be repaid.

---

117 Sheila Farr, "Starbucks: The Early Years," *HistoryLink.org*, February 15, 2017.

118 "Our Activism," *The Body Shop,* accessed October 13, 2020.

However, the assumption here is that their initial investment will increase in value as the company continues to operate using the capital to expand and become more efficient. Angel investors are typically wealthy individuals who are investing their own money in your company. Sometimes, you can get an investment by a group of angels as well. Venture capital comes from VC firms that offer very large investments for an equally large equity exchange with a side of expectations of high rates of return on equity, typically a tenfold return upon sale of the startup or IPO.

The advantage of equity capital is that it provides the significant funding entrepreneurs need to scale their business quickly. These investors offer a large influx of capital with no expectation of personal repayment and mentorship, knowledge, and network that can certainly help your business grow faster than if you were doing it alone. This is true of both angel investors and venture capitalists.

The disadvantage of equity capital is that you cede a portion of control in the decision-making regarding your company. A venture capital firm is looking to maximize its investment in your company and there is an outsized focus on value in terms of growth and profitability. This is a firm that has one goal, which is to eventually have an exit that is worth at least ten times their initial investment. This interest in your company can swiftly and easily change the direction of the company or the way the company operates.

PayJoy is one company among many that is backed by venture capital money. This FinTech start-up has gone through multiple rounds of funding since its inception. Starting with a seed round of funding of $2.3 million dollars in 2015, they then raised another $18 million in their Series A round: $8.5 million from Union Square Ventures, $4 of venture debt from Western Technology Investment, and $5.7 million of private lending capital in 2016. In 2019, they raised another $18 million in Series B from Greylock Partners, a venture capital firm that focuses on early stage startups in the consumer and enterprise software space. With this money, PayJoy is able to continue to expand their business globally to reach the 2.3 billion people all over the world in South America, Asia, and Africa and offer smartphone accessibility and financial services.[119]

WHICH FUNDING OPTION IS BEST FOR YOU?

With all of these different options, entrepreneurs really need to sit down and answer these questions:

Do I need to raise money?
How much money do I need?
What do I need it for?
Am I comfortable with debt?
Am I comfortable with giving away ownership of my company?
What does my company stand for?
Where is the value in my company?
What are the implications to my business for each of these options for funding?
Am I a social impact company?

---

[119] Akiyode-Lawanson, "Our Goal Is."

PayJoy is servicing those in need and providing services that have the opportunity to entirely change someone's life. Access to a smartphone and credit is pivotal in creating wealth, advancing professionally, and overall increasing your standard of living. With this in mind, I see PayJoy as a company that has a mission to create positive social impact and change in the world. With this goal in mind, I fundamentally understand why PayJoy is trying to raise money. It is expensive to operate in countries all around the world and they need the funding to expand globally. However, I was curious about why venture capitalists who expect profitability would invest in a company that is servicing primarily individuals in financial need?

Two thoughts come to mind. While there are clearly profits to be made, since customers must pay interest on these smartphones, there couldn't be enough to offer the VC firms a tenfold return. So, PayJoy has one option, which is to change their business model to allow for more profitability which would be counterintuitive to their social impact mission. Or, option two, they will finance those specific operations in a different way.

Speaking with Professor Alan Ross, who teaches *The Social, Political, and Ethical Environment of Business* at UC Berkeley Haas School of Business, he remarks, "Sometimes the initial investors have this great idea, right? And, [then] they bring in outside money. And, when the outside money comes in, those people aren't patient and want a big return tomorrow. All of a sudden you see things shift." Nobody was kidding when they said money talks. Therefore, it is as important who chooses to invest in you as it is who you allow to invest in you. Choose correctly and you can have a partner for life who connects you with a strategic network and funds your dreams. Choose incorrectly and your business can change before your very eyes and you might not have any control over it.

PayJoy went with option two. According to a Reuters article, "In most markets the startup does not provide financing itself, but partners with retailers and credit providers. Partners include Telefonica, Vodacom and Orange SA."[120] By partnering with major telecommunications companies, they are able to reach ten different countries around the world and gain major exposure by partnering with the biggest telecommunications players in the game without having to change their business model. The venture capital money would be used for securing more partnerships like these, developing new technologies, and helping with expansion. It's a win-win on the funding front as long as nothing drastic changes.

Ultimately, every firm has to make a funding decision just like PayJoy did. Given all of these options, every entrepreneur faces benefits and costs, literally and figuratively. It is a tightrope to walk as you balance what you need and what you are willing to give up. And while there is no right answer, the right funding option can catapult your start-up into a major company. However, the wrong funding option can be a financial disaster commercially and personally. For a business operating internationally, funding is even more important as international travel and international shipping will eat away at costs more than local or national operations. With

---

[120] Anna Irrera, "U.S. Smartphone Financing Tech Startup PayJoy Raises $20 Million," *Reuters*, May 23, 2019.

limited funds and what may seem like an infinite number of needs, entrepreneurs must carefully make this decision. Doug Ricket, Mark Heynen, and Gib Lopez certainly did.

PART 2

INSPIRED STRATEGY

CHAPTER 6

CRATE & BARREL

"Approach each customer with the idea of helping him or her solve a problem or achieve a goal, not of selling a product or service."

BRIAN TRACY[121]

HEADING TO THE CARIBBEAN ISLANDS

"If you want something done right, do it yourself."

We have all heard that quote, but Gordon and Carole Segal took it to heart. Like other twenty-three-year-olds, they had no money. Unlike other twenty-three-year-olds, they decided that wasn't going to stop them from pursuing their dreams.

In entrepreneurship classes, the professor will always ask you, "What's your value proposition?" In other words, what makes your product or service special? Different? Unique?

---

[121] Kieran Abbott, "Approach Each Customer with the Idea of Helping Him or Her Solve a Problem or Achieve a Goal, Not of Selling a Product or Service," *Dream Sight*, accessed February 18, 2021.

Why would people buy from you? Sometimes the answer is, "I'm selling a product that no one has seen before." Other times the answer is, "I do this aspect better than my competitors." But the most compelling answer I have heard is, "My product or service solves a problem."

Crate & Barrel's success and value proposition lay in the fact that not only did they operate in a different manner than their competitors, but because of this differentiation in process they made their products more affordable than anyone else in the market. By figuring out a way to solve their own problem of acquiring beautiful European furniture, they were able to solve *everyone else's* problem of acquiring that same beautiful European furniture too. This is the story of how they went from dreamers to entrepreneurs, and the beginning of Crate &Barrel's expansion from one store in 1972 to over one hundred stores now.

From the start, Gordon and Carole Segal had taste that exceeded their budget. Just like college students, many don't have a ton of money and eat instant ramen. They don't eat it because it's good, they eat it because they're broke. But that doesn't mean they don't want Michelin star quality food. In the same way, Gordon and Carole Segal wanted a living space with color palettes that popped against wooden frames and Danish stainless silverware. However, without the money to pay for it, they put it to the back of their minds.

Until their honeymoon.

They got married in 1961, and the wedding gifts they received were not quite what they envisioned. "For our wedding gifts, we didn't really get any of the kinds of things we loved. We shopped at department stores and would see beautiful Dansk designs and Danish looks and whatever, and none of our relatives had the money or the taste to buy us those kinds of wedding gifts," Gordon recalls.[122]

Then, for their honeymoon, they vacationed in the Caribbean. While they were enjoying the beach and the sun, they were more interested in the furniture stores they passed. When they were in the Virgin Islands, Carole found a Danish 1888 Stainless place setting for $295 and she was ecstatic. Those plates could not be found in the United States for anything close to that price.[123]

"It's so much more expensive in America," Carole exclaimed. She just had to know how this was possible. The merchant told her, "We have salesmen from Europe come here and we buy direct from factories."[124]

In America, all the imported European furniture got there with the help of a middleman. The middleman takes a cut out of the transaction they help barter and that's what drives the price up for customers. The furniture stores then take another cut after that. Eventually, all of these price hikes get transferred to the customer. So, at that time, only the wealthy got to buy the beautiful European furniture, and, for everyone else, it really wasn't attainable.

---

122 Guy Raz, "Crate & Barrel: Gordon Segal," February 19, 2017, in *How I Built This with Guy Raz*, produced by NPR, podcast, 1:56.

123 Raz, "Crate & Barrel: Gordon Segal," 2:39.

124 Raz, "Crate & Barrel: Gordon Segal," 2:43.

When the couple came back from their honeymoon, they not only brought back to Chicago a number of pieces they found on the Caribbean Islands, but also the knowledge to feed their expensive taste for interior design.

HOW DO YOU SOLVE PROBLEMS?

At the time, Carole was a first-grade schoolteacher and Gordon was in the real estate business, but they both had an entrepreneurship gene. Her family owned a retail and apparel store, and his family owned a restaurant. They had watched their families run businesses since they were both children, so they understood how fast-paced and busy that life can be.

Gordon craved more excitement. One day, he was washing one of the plates they bought in the Virgin Islands when he said, "There have got to be other young people like ourselves with good taste and no money. We should open a store."[125] Carole agreed with him.

Obviously, they wanted to sell beautiful furniture. After all, that was the problem that they had been facing as well. But Gordon recognized that their solution to the problem wasn't just to sell upscaled home goods, but also to sell them at a price better than all of their competitors. "If we could buy things from Europe directly and mark them up normally as if you bought them domestically, that would take a big margin, a strong margin [off]. We could offer dramatically better pricing, a more unique product that people had never

---

125 Raz, "Crate & Barrel: Gordon Segal," 3:10.

seen before," Gordon explained in a podcast interview with Guy Raz.[126]

From this idea, they started exploring in Chicago. They visited Scandinavian trade commissioners and talked to traveling salesmen. They looked through catalogs upon catalogs and received samples. In fact, the Danish trade commissioner had referred them to people they might want to visit who sold specialty items like glassware.[127]

After a period of browsing, it was time to buy inventory. It's important to remember at this point, they were both twenty-three. They had no money to their name, just a small amount of savings and their wedding gifts. Carole's father offered to buy her a car after her graduation from Northwestern University to which I imagine she said, "No, thank you. I'll take the money." They had only $10,000 between them.[128] Gordon knew it wasn't enough. He estimated that they would need double to open the store, so he went around to everyone he knew that had any kind of wealth and offered 50 percent of the company for $10,000. In 1962, venture capital didn't really exist, and no one was ready to bite on his offer. Eventually, his father loaned him $7,000. Now they had $17,000 to work with.

What was the money for? Ten thousand dollars went into stocking inventory, and everything else went toward renting and building the store. Even at that time, $17,000 really wasn't

---

126 Raz, "Crate & Barrel: Gordon Segal," 4:20.
127 Raz, "Crate & Barrel: Gordon Segal," 4:52.
128 Raz, "Crate & Barrel: Gordon Segal," 6:02.

that much money, and the Segals knew it. This period of time could only best be described as scrappy.

Gordon's dad referred them to an old elevator factory that was moving away in Chicago's Old Town district. The place was damaged, and the walls were torn up. But it only cost $350 per month to rent and they really needed the space, so they signed a three-year lease and that was that.[129] By the time it was all said and done; it was already November 15th and they had planned on opening in December. They only had three weeks to get the shop up and running.

So, how did the Segals turn this run-down elevator factory into a Scandinavian furniture haven? They rolled up their sleeves and started hammering. Those three weeks were filled with sounds of banging, clanking, and grunts of human labor. They bought crating lumber to mask the battered walls and nailed in shelves to display fixtures. They even hand-sanded the floors themselves. To say the least, it didn't look like the most furnished furniture store you could ever walk into, but it was rustic and welcoming and that was all that mattered.

"We were just enthusiastic. The value of being very young is you have a lot of energy and passion and no wisdom. Being that young was a great advantage. We had no children. We were twenty-three and had all the energy in the world" was how Gordon described that time.[130]

---

129 Raz, "Crate & Barrel: Gordon Segal," 5:39.
130 Raz, "Crate & Barrel: Gordon Segal," 8:17.

They didn't have money to buy displays, so they had the idea to just use what they have. All of their merchandise was coming in Swedish pine crates, so Gordon just flipped all of them and used the crates to display the merchandise that was imported in them. He did the same thing with the French barrels full of china. They didn't have a ton of variety in the beginning. Carole just had a great eye for furniture and the two of them would go through 1-1/2 to 2-inch catalogs. They narrowed it down to "four dinnerware patterns, [and] a very narrow selection of merchandise" for the opening day.[131]

Two weeks before the store was set to open, they still didn't have a name for it. One day, their friend came in to look around the store. Gordon was in the basement doing paperwork when Carole walked down and said, "Our friends suggest we call this place barrel and crate but Gordon, maybe, we should call it Crate & Barrel, I think that's better."[132] And that's what remained.

Crate & Barrel's Old Town location has a decades long tradition called the Christmas Walk where patrons head to the local commercial area to check out the holiday festivities. The Segals timed Crate & Barrel's opening to that particular weekend.

"We opened that first Friday of the Christmas Walk and we forgot to buy a cash register. We actually used a cigar box. It wasn't until the following Monday or Tuesday that my father

---

131 Raz, "Crate & Barrel: Gordon Segal," 7:54.
132 Raz, "Crate & Barrel: Gordon Segal," 9:02.

actually found an old NCR cash register. The ones that you used to have to [crank to get them open]" Gordon said.[133]

But the cash register wasn't the only mistake the Segals made. One of their merchandisers didn't send them the invoice for the inventory until after Christmas and the Segals had never priced furniture before. They ended up selling half of their initial merchandise *at cost*. Even still, that first month, they made a cool $8,000.

Excited, Gordon assumed that every month would be like Christmas season and he projected his sales numbers for the year to be $100,000.[134] Gordon was about to get a wake-up call.

The next month, January 1963, Crate & Barrel made $4,000. Then, in February, they made $2,000. In fact, that month "there was one day where we did $8," Gordon recalled.[135] Determined not to lose their own money and their father's money, Gordon and Carole persevered. Spring came, the weather got warmer, gaslights were put up in front of the store on the street: things were looking up for Crate & Barrel. Their name was getting its way across town and Gordon recalled people saying, "Boy, did you see that counter-culture store down on North Wells Street? They are selling nice things out of crates and barrels!"[136] That first year they ended

---

133 Raz, "Crate & Barrel: Gordon Segal," 9:31.
134 Raz, "Crate & Barrel: Gordon Segal," 10:05.
135 Raz, "Crate & Barrel: Gordon Segal," 10:24.
136 Raz, "Crate & Barrel: Gordon Segal," 10:45.

up doing $96,000. The second year, they more than doubled it and made around $200,000 in sales.

But it wasn't quite smooth sailing from there just yet. Crate & Barrel had one more hurdle to jump. In 1965, Crate & Barrel was losing their lease. Their landlord had a girlfriend who wanted the space to open a candy store, Carole remembers. Luckily, one of their two landlords "had partial interest in a piece of property down the street and couldn't find the heirs to the rest of the title."[137] Gordon leveraged his real estate expertise and described the transaction like this, "I found the lost titleholders and was able to keep the property from going into foreclosure. We got a $65,000 bank loan to build a store on the land, which we paid off in ten years. We paid rent to the landlord and eventually bought the building."

Aided by the fact that America was getting richer, more people were willing to buy nice furniture and food culture was beginning to be refined in America. Julia Childs introduced French cooking to the United States in the early 1960s and from there popularized home cooking, which directly translated into higher sales of kitchen products, silverware, and dining tables and chair sets. All things which boosted sales of Crate & Barrel to $300,000 in their third year.

LET'S GO TO EUROPE.
With more experience and money under their belt, Gordon and Carole could focus less on the nitty gritty details

---

137 Dinah Eng, "Crate & Barrel's 50 Year 'Fun Run,'" *CNN Money*, accessed September 9, 2020.

of running a business and get back to the magic of finding beautiful furniture. As they were importing more quantity and more diverse pieces, which made their way through the Saint Lawrence Seaway in Chicago, they were also getting more and more curious about where their favorite pieces were from and who made them.

In 1964, they were ready to source their furniture up close and personal rather than through a catalog. They took off to Europe for three weeks, buying the things that caught their eyes as they traipsed through the continent. The first country they went to was Belgium, where they found a glass factory that they fell in love with.[138] Then they crossed the border to Germany and attended trade fairs in Frankfurt and Cologne. After that, they met an agent in Sweden who connected them to more vendors and factories that would later on become trade partners. Finally, they made their way to Copenhagen, Denmark, where they met Torben Orskov, who sold timeless mid-century homeware. This business partnership turned into a true friendship as Torben Orskov "introduced us to Marimekko and introduced us to a lot of Danish factories. He sold us beautiful product also, wooden things and textiles and leather goods. This guy influenced our lives. He and his wife remained [our] friends for the next fifty years."[139]

The remarkable part about their success in importing European goods was that the pieces the Segals loved were made by small manufacturers and individual artisans. These are two groups of people who really were not inclined to

---

138 Raz, "Crate & Barrel: Gordon Segal," 15:28.
139 Raz, "Crate & Barrel: Gordon Segal," 16:45.

work with a pair of Americans who were following in the footsteps of unreliable American department store buyers. Many European manufacturers didn't trust American buyers because there were just so many horror stories of orders being cancelled and no reorders after they had expanded manufacturing capacity. This kind of uncertainty wasn't good for business, wasn't good for the bottom line. Gordon and Carole had to break through to these European merchants and show that they weren't like other American department store buyers.

Gordon and Carole didn't just approach these merchants with letters of credibility and money; they also came with a determination. Even if it took multiple trips without purchasing a single piece, they knew they had to forge these relationships to build the trust necessary for these European merchants to sell to them. That investment of time would allow Crate & Barrel to sell exquisite one-of-a-kind pieces not found in America at the time, and that was priceless.

One perfect example of this is the relationship the Segals developed with Gerard Hofmann, also known as Gérard le Potier, an artisan from Savoy, France, selling Savoyard pottery who is "now onto the fourth generation of people who buy [his] pottery."[140] Gordon Segal recounts the beginnings of his relationship with Hofmann, "We spent two entire days with Gerard Hofmann, a wonderful French potter living down on the Cote d'Azur, and got nowhere. On the third

---

140 "Meet Gerard the Potter," *Morzine Avoriaz*, accessed September 11, 2020.

day, he finally agreed to sell [to us]—probably just so we'd leave him alone."[141]

Gordon and Carole's trips to Europe didn't just literally influence the furniture they sold in their store; it also influenced *the way* they sold the furniture. In Europe, they would walk the cobblestone streets and marvel at the window displays of all the specialty stores they passed. This kind of display didn't exist in the United States yet, but you can be sure that they took this product placement strategy home with them.

No longer would the Crate & Barrel store's windows be just a normal window for people to peer into. Now, Carole would use it as a stage. She took cues from the Europeans on the best lighting, use of color, and, most importantly, storefront displays. Retail is all about what you see, and Carole made it so that you not only saw what the furniture was but also what it could be. She would arrange model pieces and furniture according to inspiring interior design that emulates the setting of a home. It was all in an effort to make customers feel comfortable and creative. That couch over there didn't just have to be that couch over there; it could be the centerpiece of their living room. Their furniture displays weren't individual pieces of furniture, they were arranged to look like a gorgeous room featuring their whole collection. This strategy of displaying a unified set of pieces is called *vignette*. Carole pioneered it in the United States.

---

141 Joseph P. Khan, "Crate & Barrel in 1985: A Startup on Display," *Inc.*, November 1, 1985.

Crate & Barrel sold the things that Gordon and Carole Segal would want in their own home, which meant that it was great quality, aesthetically pleasing, and exciting. Americans finally got the chance to buy furniture that was more than just functional; it was aesthetically pleasing too. And the best part, it was affordable luxury.

Who would have known that a honeymoon in the Caribbean would have led to one hundred+ stores and an upscale furniture conglomerate? No one. But, without that trip to the Caribbean and the subsequent travels to Europe, Crate & Barrel wouldn't be what it is today.

LUXURY AS BRANDING

Make no mistake about it, Crate & Barrel is a luxury brand because luxury goods are luxury goods no matter if it is coming out of a crate or a barrel. Back in the 1960s Carole and Gordon Segal opened this store as a way to purchase expensive European furniture and homeware that they wouldn't have been able to afford otherwise. The distinction between Crate & Barrel with the high-end brands that existed was simply that Crate & Barrel cut out the middleman so *its prices were slightly less expensive for the same high-quality aesthetic home goods*. This was their branding, "mass luxury."[142]

If you have taken an economics class, you know about the concept of a demand curve. Todd Fitch, Microeconomics Professor at the UC Berkeley Haas School of Business

---

142 Michael J. Silverstein and Neil Fiske, "Luxury for the Masses," *Harvard Business Review*, accessed September 11, 2020.

explained that the lower the price of a good, the greater the amount of it consumers will buy. The more expensive something is, the less you buy of it, but the cheaper it is, the more you buy of it. Simple. Straightforward. But, is that always true? What happens when you get a raise? Do you go out and buy your first Mercedes-Benz or buy the equivalent value in secondhand cars?

Obviously, demand is a bit more nuanced, and it's because of the concept of elasticity, which is far more interesting. Elasticity is all about sensitivity. Boiled down to a question, economists are asking with a given change in price, what is the corresponding change in demand? For example, with a $5 increase in price, most people (me included) would still be willing to pay for one night at a five-star hotel. This would indicate an inelastic good. But, if we were talking about a $5 increase in the price of an apple, you can bet I will be putting the apples back on the shelf and grabbing bananas instead. This would be an elastic good.

Crate & Barrel sells inelastic goods. Luxury goods are coveted and aren't easily substitutable, so if prices get bumped, no one bats an eye. But here is the most interesting thing about luxury goods: As a consumer's income rises, they will demand luxury goods at a rate that surpasses the rate of their increase in income. Let me give you an example. If you went from making $80,000 a year to $1 million a year, the rate at which you buy McDonald's won't go up by that much. But the rate at which you go out to restaurants with $$$$ on Yelp would increase pretty significantly from before.

So, the question now is, why? Why do we want to buy extravagant things? I think it's because, ultimately, it makes us feel special. And, making customers feel special has been a crucial reason for Crate & Barrel's success. Hannes Gurzki, an expert on branding, marketing, and luxury and a program director at the European School of Management and Technology, Germany identified three reasons how luxury brands create desire:

1. *Creating the Extraordinary*: Luxury goods make us feel like we are a part of an exclusive club. It offers great amenities and services, but we had to jump through hoops to get there. "We rarely desire what we can have immediately. That's why we seldom desire the ordinary world. Desire is created when something is just out of reach," Gurzki explains.[143]
2. *Creating Distance*: Luxury goods are framed to be fantastic and outside of normal realities. Have you ever seen a Hermes commercial shot in a subway? (Not hating on the NY Subway. I love the subway. I'm just saying). No. Who wants to aspire to be the person sweating in a dark tunnel waiting for a train after a nine-hour workday? Companies like Hermes intentionally shoot their commercials in places like the manicured gardens of Versailles because we can all dream about living in a French palace, for a couple days at the least, no matter who you are.[144]
3. *Building a Dream*: In the game of effectiveness, showing is always better than telling. Luxury brands succeed at

---

143 Hannes Gurzki, "Dreaming up a World – How Luxury Brands Create Desire," *Forbes*, accessed September 11, 2020.
144 *PegaseBuzz*, "Hermès—Bandanas de Soie [Commercial 2014]," July 11, 2014, video, 1:30.

creating an environment and story that allows customers to create their own fantasies within that luxurious world. High-end wedding dresses tap into this literally. White fabric is not just white fabric; it's a gateway for a fairy tale day.

From its inception, Crate & Barrel checked off all three of these boxes and this is why customers keep coming back for more to this very day.

1. The Segals had a personal journey of not being able to obtain beautiful quality European furniture and opened a store to put these products within reach of Americans. Most young couples couldn't just buy the furniture on the spot, but they could certainly wait a month or two months to save up the money to buy an extraordinary piece of furniture they want.
2. The Segals literally created distance by sourcing their products not only from a different continent but also local artisans. European furniture wasn't really common in the 1960s, so all of the furniture Crate & Barrel was selling was outside of normal reality. This only got heightened when they began their tours through every European country finding antique wood homeware in Denmark and artisanal pottery in France.
3. Carole built a dream by introducing "vignette," the act of displaying a complete room, be it a bedroom or dining table, with all the collection of pieces together. She was showing her customers that their rooms may not look like this at home, but if they buy Crate & Barrel furniture, their rooms can look like that in the future. And she got this idea of vignette from her trips across Europe.

Crate & Barrel's existence in the luxury space was crucial to their future success. They started selling a dream, albeit a relatively affordable one, in a remodeled elevator factory. But it was their charm, priority of customer experience, and commitment to selling exquisite one-of-a-kind furniture that convinced their customers that when they buy from Crate & Barrel, they are getting something special. As a luxury brand, Crate & Barrel offered an experience unlike any other European furniture at rates you couldn't find anywhere else in America. As a result, they sold their customers not just furniture, but a dream. And this, in turn, is what makes Crate & Barrel special.

CHAPTER 7

STARBUCKS

"Travel makes one modest. You see what a tiny place you occupy in the world."

GUSTAVE FLAUBERT[145]

What started as an ordinary business trip turned into a passion that changed the world.

THE ORIGINAL HISTORY OF HOWARD SCHULTZ AT STARBUCKS

Between 1981 and 1983, Howard Schultz went on two business trips. One to Seattle and one to Italy. Without these trips, the world might not have Starbucks as we know it today. Obviously, America had coffee in the 1900s, but America didn't have *Starbucks* until 1983.

(Imagine that, if everyone could find the next billion-dollar idea from a few quick trips, wouldn't that be nice.)

---

145 "Quotable Quote," *Goodreads*, accessed August 26, 2020.

At this point, you might be thinking, what is she talking about? Starbucks is American. Starbucks is a home-grown, American coffee brand founded in 1971. You're not wrong, but you are missing the point. While Starbucks is definitely an American brand, the premise of the Starbucks that we love today is Italian.

In 1971, Starbucks was a *coffee bean* company. The three original founders: Gordon Bowker, Jerry Baldwin, and Zev Siegl were three friends who graduated from the University of San Francisco and all shared a love for high-quality espresso beans.[146] Taken under the wing of Alfred Peet, who is the founder of Peet's Coffee, they were inspired by what Peet taught them regarding the intricacies of roasting coffee beans. The original Starbucks under these three friends sold *only* high-quality coffee beans and coffee brewing equipment for the home. They believed that the true beauty of Starbucks would be the rich aroma of coffee filling up *patrons' homes*. Nobody could predict what would happen after Howard Schultz would come across this coffee commodity business.

At the time, Howard Schultz was working for Hammarplast, a Swedish household goods company. Starbucks was purchasing their drip coffee machines in quantities Howard Schultz had never seen before.[147] How could it be that a small operation in Seattle, Washington, was ordering more coffee machines than their largest customer, Macy's? This

---

146 Sheila Farr, "Starbucks: The Early Years," *HistoryLink.org*, February 2, 2017

147 Guy Raz, "Live Episode! Starbucks: Howard Schultz," September 27, 2017, in *How I Built This with Guy Raz*, produced by NPR, podcast, 12:45.

was the first indication that Starbucks had something really special going on.

In 1981, Howard Schultz walked into the original Starbucks on Pike's Place and smelled the earthy aroma of coffee beans and magic in the air. At that moment, something clicked. The three founders introduced him to the story of coffee and walked him through the roasting plant. During this time, Starbucks displayed the coffees, teas, and spices sold at the store and only allowed brew coffee as a sample.[148] Like it was a fairy tale, Schultz was enchanted by Starbucks. "I can't explain it. But I knew I was in a special place, and the product kind of spoke to me," Schultz said of the experience.[149]

Most people, when encountering a store that they really like, turn into customers or loyal patrons. Not Schultz. He didn't want to just be a customer of Starbucks, he wanted to be a part of this *coffee bean* company. After a year of persuading the owners and pounding on doors saying, "If you want to expand the company, I think I can help you," Schultz was brought on in 1982 as Director of Retail Operations and Marketing for a coffee company that strictly sells great coffee beans.[150] At the time, Schultz was committed to this mission. But things change as time goes on and horizons broaden. For Schultz, the horizons literally broadened.

---

148 Farr, "Starbucks: The Early Years."

149 Biography.com Editors, "Howard Schultz Biography," *A&E Television Networks,* updated September 9, 2019.

150 Raz, "Live Episode!," 14:25.

INTERNATIONAL TRAVEL, CULTURE, AND CUPS OF ESPRESSO

In 1983, Starbucks sent Schultz on a business trip to Milan, Italy, for a trade show. This was his very first time visiting Italy and he was struck by the hundreds of espresso bars that seemed to be on every street corner. But it wasn't just the fact that there were so many espresso bars that enchanted him, it was more so the romance and theatre that was happening in each espresso bar that really piqued his interest.

Explaining his epiphany in Milan during a live interview with Guy Raz on *How I Built This*, he said "When I was walking the streets of Milan, every twenty or thirty yards you are intercepted, literally, with an Italian coffee bar. And I walked into all of these places and kept seeing the theatre, the romance, and the nectar of the gods, which was espresso."[151] What he realized after going to the same coffee shop at the same time every day was that he was seeing the same people. He had inadvertently joined a community centered around espresso coffee. "I started realizing this is a third place between home and work. But the beverage was the draw. So, I realized while I was in Italy, Starbucks was in the coffee business but perhaps, in the wrong part of the business. And I raced back with such enthusiasm and such passion that I overwhelmed them when I got back."[152]

There was a sense of community with each person who passed into the espresso bar to say hello to his or her fellow neighbor. It was beautiful, and it didn't exist in America.

---

151 Raz, "Live Episode!," 15:31.
152 Raz, "Live Episode!," 16:07.

When Americans think of coffee, we think of drip coffee, cold milk, and, most importantly, a to-go cup. We go in to grab a coffee and have no expectation of speaking to the person on our right. In Italy, coffee is a ritual of "drinking coffee, standing up at a bar, chatting with the barista", and *never* taking it to- go.[153] Italian coffee culture is serious and can only best be described by an Italian.

Elizabeth Minchilli, an Italian American author who has written six books on Italian food and drink, explains coffee as an experience. To the Italians, it's not what you consume but also how you consume it. As you travel from Naples to Florence to Milan to Palermo, each cappuccino you drink may taste a bit different in coffee notes or temperature. However, the culture and the rituals that are abided by remain the same no matter where you go.

Here is what a standard coffee day for an Italian looks like:

8:30 a.m.: Walk to coffee bar one on the way to work and enjoy a macchiato as you wave to your barista
8:45 a.m.: Work
10:30 a.m.: Coffee Break at a different bar close to work and you drink a cappuccino
10:45 a.m.: Work
12:00 p.m.: Lunch
1:00 p.m.: Work
4:00 p.m.: Second Coffee Break at a bar close to work where you have your final cup of espresso

---

153 Sylvia Poggioli, "Italy's Coffee Culture Brims with Rituals and Mysterious Rules," *NPR*, July 14, 2017.

4:15 p.m.: Work
6:30 p.m.: Finish Work and eat Dinner

What's special about this schedule doesn't lie in the fact that Italians drink a lot of coffee; it lies in the particularities of their coffee, down to the very time they drink it. In the morning and around lunchtime, a heavier coffee drink like a cappuccino or a macchiato hit the spot. But by late afternoon, something that *pesano* (which means heavy in Italian) might not sit well in the stomach, so you switch to a cup of espresso. Like I said, coffee isn't just a drink in Italy, it's a way of life.

But what coffee is to be drunk at a certain time isn't the only habit that Italians practice; they also extend this courtesy to where they drink their coffee. Minchilli says, "I think everybody in Italy has their own sort of favorite place they go to for coffee." Maybe it serves the coffee that delights their tastebuds the most. Maybe it's the closest one to the house. Or, maybe, it's the childhood coffee bar that was their parent's go-to. Whatever the reason, every Italian has a favorite and they visit it like clockwork. There is no switching coffee bars. There is no, "I want a change of scenery." And there is a very specific reason for this.

Minchilli says, "You are always there and, let's say, kind of your life. Every day you get to see the same people. It's almost like a private club. You get to know about the people and check in with them, 'How was your trip? How is your work?'. It's more than just talking about the weather. It's very much so about where you are and what you're doing currently."

This is community.

In America, chances are that on any given day, nobody in any given coffeehouse has ever even seen the other patrons who are sharing that space. Generally, nobody walks into a coffeehouse in the United States looking forward to their conversations with either the barista or other patrons. Everybody is craving their morning jolt, their cup of joe.

This is what Howard Schultz wanted to change. Americans drink coffee, but he felt as though they miss out on the magic. Coffee doesn't just have to be about the rich, hearty aroma of perfectly roasted coffee beans or that addictive first sip that gets you get out of bed in the morning. It can be about the experience of sharing time and company with people who love coffee just as much as you do.

BUYING STARBUCKS

So from there, Schultz made it his mission to bring this coffee magic to Starbucks. He went back to the owners and said, "I see the future of the business. We have to transform Starbucks and bring out espresso."[154] Instead of strictly selling packaged coffee beans for coffee drinkers to brew by themselves, he wanted to bring the coffee to them.

As unthinkable as it is now, his idea wasn't an instant hit. The owners didn't really share his vision and wanted to focus on the coffee beans as they always had. Starbucks was by no means doing poorly, with six stores already and more in the works. They were expanding as a commodity business,

---

154 *The Corp With A-Rod and Big Cat*, "Howard Schultz Talks Starbucks, Baseball, and Supersonics with A-Rod & Barstool Big Cat—The Corp," September 24, 2019, video, 12:36.

selling the highest quality coffee beans for the consumers to enjoy in their homes.

But Schultz was nothing if not persistent. He finally convinced the owners to let him open up a coffee bar at their newest location in Seattle. In 1985, the very first Starbucks Caffe Latte was served in downtown Seattle, not Pike's Place. This new coffeehouse was a hit. With hundreds of customers coming in for a freshly brewed cup of high-quality coffee, this left an impression on Schultz. But it didn't quite leave the same mark on the three original owners. Unfortunately, Howard said, "It was so successful that it completely dwarfed the other side of the business. The two founders at the time did not like the disproportionate level of sales and how the store was functioning. And they respectfully said to me, 'We don't want to repeat this.'"[155]

They didn't think of Starbucks as a coffeehouse; they thought of Starbucks as a commodity business. They had their sights on buying Peet's Coffee, another coffee bean company at the time, which meant there was no cash to keep funding Schultz's vision to expand Starbucks as a coffeehouse.

To Schultz's credit, he believed in this concept so much that if he had to do it himself, he was willing to. And so, he did. He left Starbucks in 1985 to found his own coffee bar, Il Giornale, named after the Italian word for newspaper. Schultz was serious about recreating the authentic espresso bars that had inspired him on that trip to Milan. That wonderful journey to Italy was about to lead Schultz on a much more difficult

---

155 Raz, "Live Episode!," 17:47.

journey. While trying to open Il Giornale, Schultz was met with obstacles the whole way through.

First came the money problems. To open stores, he needed to raise money. The first investors he got on board were, ironically, the founders of Starbucks. When Schultz quit his job to pursue this dream, they said, "Well if you do that, we'd like to invest in you."[156] In return for a $200,000 investment, Il Giornale was to use Starbucks coffee beans. And, the kicker is that in the contract, they put in a clause saying that Schultz had to raise $600,000 in outside money to be able to use their $200,000.[157] When it all came to, Howard Schultz talked to two hundred forty-two investors and most of them said, "No."

He remembers "people [saying], 'Let me try and understand this. The name of the company is something no one can pronounce. You're going to sell coffee for $2 to $3 a cup in a paper cup with Italian names that no one has ever heard of. And you want to give healthcare to your employees.'"[158] It really was a tough sell. It wasn't until his wife Sheri Schultz's best friend, Carol and her husband said, "We don't need any pitch, we are just going to trust you" and gave Schultz a check for $100,000 before the money ball got rolling.[159]

Second came the authenticity problems. Il Giornale wasn't facing complaints that the store wasn't authentic enough; customers were complaining that it was *too* authentic. When

---

156 Raz, "Live Episode!," 18:46.
157 Raz, "Live Episode!," 20:35.
158 Raz, "Live Episode!," 20:50.
159 Raz, "Live Episode!," 21:35.

Il Giornale first opened, they played Italian opera, mandated their baristas to wear white button-ups and bowties, and did not provide a seating area.[160]

But, America is not Italy as Il Giornale would quickly learn from subsequent complaints. Morning patrons didn't expect or want to hear vibrato against an orchestra at seven in the morning. Nor did they appreciate the fact that they were expected to stand their entire time at the store. Quickly, Il Giornale changed the music, moved in tables and chairs, and started offering to-go cups.

Fortunately, what Il Giornale didn't have a problem with was capturing the magic that so enchanted Schultz during his first trip to Milan. Here, customers can see their baristas pressing the coffee grinds, freshly brewing a steaming delicious latte, and pouring it into a ceramic cup. This was the theatre of coffee, a drink not meant to simply be enjoyed by the tastebuds, but by the eyes and nose as well.

Rituals were beginning to form. The drink was drunk on the spot, just like the Italians did it. In and out of the store in five minutes, patrons greeted other patrons as they waited for their coffee, drank the coffee which isn't made piping hot but instead the perfect temperature of instant consumption, and handed the cup back as they get on their merry way. These behavioral patterns fit perfectly with customers who were usually employees busy rushing to or from work who

---

160 *Hook*, "How a Poor Kid from Brooklyn Made Starbucks," March 2, 2020, video, 8:30.

just wanted their quick jolt. Sales grew, but this isn't the end of the story of the origins of Starbucks.

In 1987, Starbucks had run into financial trouble as they were deeply in debt following the purchase of Peet's Coffee Company. Jerry Baldwin and Gordon Bowker wanted to sell Starbucks. The owners couldn't think of a better person to take over the company than Schultz, so they offered him a 60-day exclusive to buy Starbucks for $3.8 million.[161] Schultz approached the original investors of Il Giornale and others pitching his idea to change the way Americans drink and interact with coffee. One month in, he had raised $1.9 million.

However, that wasn't the only thing that happened. The owners reached out to Schultz to tell him that one of his original investors cut in with an unsolicited offer to pay "$4 million, all cash, no due diligence".[162] This investor was one of Seattle's biggest businessmen at the time. What was Schultz to do? Schultz was a man with a dream and no money up against a Seattle tycoon with deep pockets. Who could blame the owners for wanting to go with the better offer? After all, who turns down an extra $200,000? Schultz felt defeated as his dream slipped away. Two days later, he was telling Scott Greenberg, his friend and lawyer at the time, what had transpired. Scott told Schultz, "You gotta go see the senior partner of our law firm tomorrow morning."[163]

---

161 *The Corp*, "Howard Schultz Talks Starbucks," 25:54.
162 *The Corp*, "Howard Schultz Talks Starbucks," 26:17.
163 *The Corp*, "Howard Schultz Talks Starbucks," 26:37.

At 8 a.m. the next day, Schultz met Bill Gates Sr. and relayed the entire story.

"Have you left anything out?" Bill Gates Sr. asks.
"No."
"Is everything you told me true?" Bill Gates Sr. asks.
"It's 100 percent truthful."
"Yes."
"Come back in two hours."[164]

Two hours later, Gates Sr. says, "Come on. We are going to go for a walk." They cross the street to see the Seattle Business titan in his office. All six-foot-seven of Bill Gates Sr. towered over the desk when he said, "You should be ashamed of yourself. You are stealing this kid's dream. So, this is what's going to happen: We are going to walk out of here, Howard is going to buy the company, and you are going to stand down."[165] Then, they walk out. Eventually, Bill Gates Sr. contacted his son Bill Gates, co-founder of Microsoft, and together with some other investors, they contributed to the $3.8 million Schultz needed to buy Starbucks' brand and six physical locations. From that moment on, Starbucks began its journey to changing the English vocabulary to include Italian coffee orders and making the term "Starbucks" synonymous with "coffee."

---

164 *The Corp*, "Howard Schultz Talks Starbucks," 26:59.
165 *The Corp*, "Howard Schultz Talks Starbucks," 27:46.

INTERNATIONAL BUSINESS AND THE PIVOT

What Howard Schultz was able to do with an idea is nothing short of extraordinary, but it is also quite accessible in the way that a trip to Italy isn't exclusive to Howard Schultz. The joy and sense of community found in Italian coffee bars had existed for ages before his trip in 1983. He just saw the opportunity in bringing this lifestyle to a new market, the United States, from a brand that people already knew and trusted.

The Starbucks that we know and love today originated from an idea borrowed from a land far away. This might sound superfluous, but boiled down to it, coffee bars were and continue to be prolific in Italy; they just didn't exist in the United States in the 1980s. Howard Schultz bridged this gap, and the only way he could have done it was *by going to Italy.*

Selling brewed coffee from a place selling coffee beans is a logical extension from a marketing point of view. What better way is there to tell customers directly, "We sell the best coffee in this fifty-mile radius. Don't believe us? Try it yourself." Starbucks had given out samples before as a way for customers to get a sneak peek of what magic lay inside the coffee bean packaging. The original founders just didn't think that commodifying those taste tests had any future. They didn't go to Italy.

Howard Schultz did. He saw firsthand that people would be willing to come into a coffee bar or coffeehouse to get their daily cups of coffee. In fact, it was the everyday meetings between baristas and patrons in Milan that he realized could be replicated in Seattle. Schultz described it best when he said, "A lot of people said [this is a crazy idea to roll out these coffee stores from coast to coast]. But we believed early on that what we had seen in Italy was replicable in America through an American lens. It was thinking: let's create a store that is not only a store for coffee but also produces a sense of community between home and work. And, early on, we realized that the brand we were about to build was experiential."[166] So what Howard Schultz did to Starbucks was to revolutionize the way they sell coffee. He did what businesspeople call a "Pivot."

In basketball, the way a player pivots is by keeping one foot firmly planted on the ground while the other foot moves, changing your direction. For the artists out there, think of a human compass. For entrepreneurs, this means keeping one aspect of your business but changing the direction of your company entirely. Jacqueline Kirtley, Wharton management professor and author of the research paper *What is a Pivot? Explaining When and How Entrepreneurial Firms Decide to Make Strategic Change and Pivot* describes a change in strategy like this: "Changing something fundamental about what the firm is doing. So, a change in the strategy might be: Are we a service company? Are we a product company? If your beliefs don't change, you don't change your strategy. You stay on course. But every once in a while, in this case, only in about twenty-one instances, they did change. They did change their beliefs about what to do, about what was going on, about what was uncertain. Their beliefs did get affected."[167]

---

166 Raz, "Live Episode!," 28:42.
167 Knowledge@Wharton, "When and How Entrepreneurs Pivot," *Knowledge@Wharton*, June 11, 2019.

Howard Schultz's business trip to Italy didn't change the fact that he wanted to sell coffee products, but it did change his beliefs. He recognized the value in changing Starbucks from a products business, selling bags of coffee beans, to a service business, selling brewed coffee and offering not just a physical product that people loved but an intangible community that people wanted to join.

When you see more, you know more. And, when you know more, you can change your mind and learn something new. For entrepreneurs who are looking for their next big idea, remember you can take a page out of Howard Schultz's book. You don't always have to start from scratch. Sometimes just changing and improving upon an existing idea is enough to be worth hundreds of millions of dollars.

CHAPTER 8

MOMOFUKU

"Entrepreneur is someone who has a vision for something and a want to create."

DANIEL KARP, CEO OF TUMBLR[168]

He was scared to walk into the Ramen Bar. It was a local spot, and he wasn't a local.

"But Japan has the BEST ramen in the world. Whatever, I'm quitting my job anyways, I want noodles," is along the lines of what David Chang thought about that time in his life.

He walked in and literally never looked back. They were in fact the best noodles he had ever eaten. A couple years later, a couple jobs later, and one entrepreneurial spirit that just won't quit later, he came up with THE idea.

But, let me start from the beginning.

---

168 Sujan Patel, "21 Success Tips for Young and Aspiring Entrepreneurs," *Entrepreneur*, accessed February 8, 2021.

Ever since David was a kid, he's been eating ramen. The original bowl was special because that's a memory filled with nostalgia. He would frequent a certain noodle restaurant in Alexandria, Virginia, with his father. He was transfixed with watching the guy making the noodles. The flour was flying, and the dough was being kneaded and folded from one ball to hundreds of strands. This was Level One Ramen, and the beginning of a lifetime obsession.

Then, when he studied abroad in London, he frequented Wagamama, a hip ramen chain.[169] Each ramen bowl consisted of freshly made ramen noodles sitting in a hearty umami broth with braised pork and all the fixings. This was Level Two ramen. And he had it all the time.

But eventually this had to end; David couldn't go to college forever. He was reaching the end of his college career grasping at straws for what he would do post-graduation. Just like many college folks then, now, and in the future, he decided to show up to the career fair. For most people, the career fair is like shopping, you go up to a booth, in this case a company table you're interested in, and you spend about five minutes there.

"Hi, my name is [insert name]. I am a fourth-year majoring in [insert major] and I'm really interested in [insert industry, career, job]. I would love to learn more about your company and this position."

---

169 Rob Patronite and Robin Raisfeld, "The I Chang," *New York*, January 12, 2007.

It's just like professional speed dating, with both sides looking for a best fit and making decisions based on initial conversations. Each industry, company, and even manager has their own special process, but one thing that remains true across the board is that no one really settles on the first person or company they see. Just like it's not common for a person to marry the first person they go on a date with.

David was different. He walked into the career fair because he was tired of not knowing what he was going to do when people asked him. He "made a right and it was a teaching English in Japan corporation."[170] The way he tells the story is that in a split second he decided, "I want a job here. They gave it to me, and I didn't think anything about it."[171] He didn't think anything of the fact that he didn't speak Japanese or didn't really want the job. In fact, he wasn't even sure he was going to go. But, the time came, he packed his bags, and he went. Little did he know, he was about to hit Level Three ramen.

RAMEN TO END ALL RAMEN

The company didn't send him to any major Japanese city like Tokyo or Sapporo, which he would have preferred. Instead, they sent him to a place he never would have chosen, "a small village called Izumi Tottori," where his "backyard was a rice paddy."[172] He didn't like it there to say the least and only

---

[170] Dax Shepard, "David Chang," April 30, 2020, in *Armchair Expert with Dax Shepard,* produced by Armchair Umbrella, podcast, 23:51.
[171] Shepard, "David Chang," 23:56.
[172] Shepard, "David Chang," 24:51.

lasted four months. However, there was one bright spot. In that village, there was a local ramen shop, a place that he had always been too afraid to go into because, well, he wasn't a local. Imagine an exclusive club where everyone around you had access and partied at. But one night, you find out there's a party. No one ever said you couldn't go, but you were clearly not invited. It *feels* like there is an invisible barrier for you. It's a hard pill to swallow when you feel like you have something to lose. At this point, he had nothing to lose. He was ready to quit his job and he had never eaten ramen from an authentic ramen shop before, let alone in Japan.

He walked in and was immediately greeted by the mouth-watering smell of rich emulsified tonkotsu broth and a scene of hard-boiled eggs in bowls.[173] Looking back on it now, this would be his enlightenment moment.

He ordered the bowl of noodles, which he would later go on to compare with instant ramen like this: "The best way I can describe it is having really bad frozen concentrated orange juice and thinking this is orange juice your entire life. And, then you get beautiful, perfect fresh squeezed. And you are like, 'Oh, shit. This is what orange juice is.'"[174]

Level Three ramen. The type of ramen so good that it unlocks a small desire to effectively ruin a father's wish that his son would never have to work in a restaurant because he knows how painstakingly hard it is. David Chang's father was not unfamiliar with the restaurant scene because he not only

---

173 Shepard, "David Chang," 25:52.
174 Shepard, "David Chang," 26:30.

worked for a restaurant before, he's also the owner of one too. His father had no idea the disappointment and eventual pride that was waiting for him in the years to come.

When David came back to New York, he shoved the cooking desire down and took a job in corporate America. He was twenty-two, sitting in an office, pushing papers, and answering phone calls. He thought, "This is what people do every day? You type on a keyboard, do some stupid shit, make some phone calls, get yelled at, and you eat dinner at your desk. And, then you go home, and you are so tired, and pray to god you don't have to go to work the next day. This is a horrible existence, and I can't do this."[175] So during this existential crisis, he took a page out of his Religion major and decided to use a concept from Catholic theologians to determine what he was supposed to do with his life.

The concept was via negativa, which is a Christian way of speaking about God and his attributes.[176] It's the idea that humans aren't capable of positively confirming anything said about God. So, the best we can describe God is by way of negation. Essentially, instead of pointing out what God is, Christians can better understand God by pointing out what God is not.

He applied this principle to his life. For some time, he decided to do several things for two or three days before quitting to do something else.[177] For example, he worked a desk job in

---

175 Shepard, "David Chang," 28:03.
176 Anna Krestyn, "What Is the via Negativa?" *Aleteia*, March 4, 2013.
177 Shepard, "David Chang," 28:55.

finance for a short period of time before realizing that was not for him. Through the process of eliminating everything he thought he could do, he landed on the one thing he always had an itch to try, cooking. So, he went to the French Culinary Institute where he honed a work ethic that nobody else could beat.[178] This would eventually come in handy but at the time was one of his most polarizing personality traits which pushed people away from him and his aggressive, stubborn personality.

It was 2000 when he graduated from culinary school and began to work as a line cook at Mercer Kitchen, which was one of Jean Georges' restaurants in New York. Then he learned that Tom Colicchio, host of *Top Chef* and co-founder of Gramercy Tavern, among other restaurants, was opening up Craft, a fine-dining restaurant in New York City. Chang knew that he wanted to eventually work at Craft, and he didn't care in what capacity. He started answering phone calls on his days off from Mercer Kitchen and slowly moved up the ranks to do knife work in the mornings he worked at Craft.[179] By the time Craft had its grand opening, he was working there full time. He might not have consciously thought it, but he was honing his skills to fulfill his dream.

FOLLOWING HIS PASSION: FOOD
Fast forward to 9/11, when he was still working at Craft. But he was shaken by the deaths of people he knew, which led to a new relationship with risk.

---

178 Shepard, "David Chang," 29:08.
179 Shepard, "David Chang," 30:51.

"I have to constantly remind myself of why I opened up a restaurant that should never have opened up, and it was because it was 2004. . . . You know, September 11th had happened. And earlier that year three of my good friends had passed away—there was just a series of tragic events in my life that help you realize just how unimportant a decision that you think is very serious is. You know, when you're talking about life and death, opening a restaurant is pretty insignificant."[180]

After Craft, David went back to Japan in hopes of tying up some "unfinished business" and ended up living and working there for two years.[181] He spent some time making noodles in an *izakaya*—a soba shop—and then worked at Tokyo's Park Hyatt Hotel. It was during this period that he not only learned more about cooking, but also about himself. Japan is an expensive place to live, notoriously so. In fact, Japan is consistently rated as having the highest average living costs in the world.[182] But he found ways to eat super cheaply there and it was great food. Often, when we think of a nice meal in America, we think white tablecloths in a French restaurant with a tasting menu. It's extravagant. It's exclusive. It's expensive.

"[In Japan], everyone is actually eating well. I ate most of my meals at convenience stores, like the 7/11 equivalent there.

---

180 David Chang, "On Guts," *Open Transcripts at Patreon*, August 25, 2013.
181 Shepard, "David Chang," 35:57.
182 "The Cost of Living in Japan," *InterNations GO!*, updated April 21, 2020.

Some of the best food I've had were in convenience stores, like sandwiches and noodles."[183]

So, when he came back to the States and started cooking at Cafe Boulud, a French restaurant on the Upper East Side with one Michelin Star, it was just in such stark contrast to the democratized good food that he found to be common in Japan.[184]

This was when he decided to "do something different, and I knew it wasn't going to be fine dining."[185]

After some time in Alexandria, VA, taking care of his mom, he returned to New York with $130,000 of start-up capital raised from his dad and friends. He was on his way to fulfill his dream of owning his own restaurant on his terms.

"Having the luxury and opportunity of living abroad, traveling abroad, all over the world, you realize that great food is amazing at all price points. And some of the best eating in the world is on the lower end."[186]

This was the beginning of Momofuku.

---

183 Shepard, "David Chang," 36:58.
184 Shepard, "David Chang," 41:45.
185 Patronite and Raisfeld, "The I Chang."
186 Chang, "On Guts."

MOMOFUKU: THE START OF IT ALL

So, what made Momofuku special? You'd have to go back to Chang's travels. He realized that all around the world, normal people were paying affordable prices for meals that in America would cost someone their whole day's paycheck. This is the essence of Momofuku.

"When I was able to travel throughout Asia, I'm eating an amazing meal for like 50 cents and I was like this is something everyone wants to experience. And that was the next epiphany, everybody wants to eat well. It's just not accessible, or it's too expensive. But it's not the case, the only place where that is not the case is America. And, I was like it doesn't have to be that way. And, that's what Momofuku was. . . . Let's do noodles and let's try to apply the same sort of discipline and technical rigor that I learned working at some of the best restaurants and apply it to $12 to $15 bowls of soup."[187]

Before David Chang committed to opening up a ramen restaurant, he was already set on its name, Momofuku. "Anything ramen became my hobby after my first trip to Japan, and I learned that the guy who created Cup O'Noodles was named Momofuku Ando."[188] Like an everyday hero, Momofuku Ando created instant ramen that most college students and non-college students alike have guilt cravings for. For David Chang, ramen couldn't have been a guilty craving, it was everything. Not only did he name his restaurant after Momofuku Ando, he also extended this name to the logo. In Japanese, Momofuku means "lucky peach." Eventually,

---

187 Shepard, "David Chang," 51:39.
188 Shepard, "David Chang," 41:26.

Chang made a little peach the face of the brand. And, he needed all the luck he could get.

His dad warned him long before he started this endeavor just how tough the restaurant industry actually is. Not to mention that $130,000 is not a lot to open a restaurant in New York City. And, to top it all off, Chang didn't have the experience to open a restaurant either. He had never run a restaurant before or even been a sous-chef. This was not a recipe for success.

But, the beauty of doing something for the first time is that you don't know what the rules are so you don't know if you are breaking any and, frankly, you don't care if you are. All David cared about was getting the restaurant up and running, no matter what. And this sort of back against the wall type situation would be enough to discourage anyone else, but it oddly fit him well. "I only know one way of getting anything done and that's throwing everything I have to a problem."[189] This was a scrappy period for Chang, but that's his strength and he had nothing to lose and everything to gain.

The first order of business for this burgeoning restaurant was to find another chef willing to work with Chang. He found this chef in Joaquin Baca, a twenty-eight-year-old cook from New Mexico who had been trying to get his foot in the door of New York City restaurants.[190]

---

189 Shepard, "David Chang," 29:42.
190 Patronite and Raisfeld, "The I Chang."

The two of them got to work. When they first opened, they were serving $7 to $10 hot and cold noodles in a bare restaurant. Food was way more important than the decor and they had a limited budget. In a choice between okay food and great decor or great food and bland decor, the latter clearly stands out. This restaurant on First Avenue was small. Stools were narrowly placed. There wasn't that much space to move around. The place was lit with functionality rather than aesthetics in mind. At the time, David Chang might not have cared all that much about how the place looked other than the fact that it had to be clean to pass health inspection, but he was deeply focused on serving great food. Momofuku was competing against the thousands of restaurants in New York City, but one in particular really dug under his skin: Sapporo East, right across the street. The competitive man Chang was, he used this as motivation, "Let's cook better than those guys, then let's raise the level from there."[191]

RAMEN TO END ALL RAMEN: PART 2

It's important to note right now that Momofuku is a ramen shop owned and operated by a man who has the deepest appreciation for Japanese ramen. Chang served great ramen, delicious ramen, mouth-watering ramen, but not authentic ramen. He would never claim that.

Ramen in Japan is what pasta is to Italy. There is nearly a ramen shop on every corner, it's so common, and each region of Japan has their own special version of this noodle dish.

---

191 Ibid.

In Hokkaido, there is the most popular version of ramen called Sapporo. Made with a miso base, seafood, and a heap of sweet corn, this bowl of ramen is salty and hearty and what we usually think of when we talk about ramen.[192]

In Fukushima, there is a much lighter version of ramen called Kitakata. Made with a soy-based broth, pork bones, and dried sardines, this bowl of ramen is gentle and clear.[193]

In Fukuoka, there is the rich bowl of noodles that many may know of as Tonkotsu but is actually called Hakata. This bowl of ramen is easily identifiable by its milky white broth. Made with pork bones and thin noodles, this bowl of ramen is served by the umami that permeates throughout.[194]

In Tokyo, there is what can be considered the original ramen called, aptly, Tokyo. Made with chicken, seafood, and soba in a dashi soup, this bowl of ramen is a clear and humble homage to Tokyo's beginnings.[195]

These are just four types of regional ramen amongst many more that show the variety and versatility of ramen that exists. But what all of these ramens have in common is that they are all cheap and highly accessible. In Japan, you can get a bowl of ramen for 600 Yen, the equivalent of $5.67. Ramen

---

192 Alethea Tan, "10 Types of Ramen and Where They Are From," *Michelin Guide Singapore*, October 2, 2017.
193 Ibid.
194 Ibid.
195 Ibid.

is the fast food of Japan but made of the quality from a gourmet restaurant.

In the very first episode of season one of *Mind of a Chef*, David Chang took Peter Meehan, a friend and colleague, to try tsukemen ramen from the place that invented it, Taishoken, which is still around today in Tokyo.[196] This is yet another variation of ramen that is characterized by the separation of broth and noodles. The broth is a bit heavier than normal broth, as it is meant to be a dipping sauce for the noodles. In the episode, we can see the two of them walking up to a vending machine wall. Instead of snacks or bottled drinks, it was pictures of ramen. For some ramen restaurants, this is their menu.

Patrons walk up, choose their bowl of ramen, insert cash into the slot on the wall, and grab their ticket. When their food is ready, they hand the ticket to the chef and the ramen is served at the table. It is easy and it is fast. When the bowl of broth, toppings, and soft-boiled egg were placed in front of Chang and Meehan, you could see the steam coming from the bowls, and with enough imagination, you could smell the rich aroma of pork too. Then, the waiter brought over the noodles and they were glistening. This is great food at affordable prices. This is what David Chang fell in love with and what he brought over to New York.

Momofuku's goal was never to bring authentic ramen to New York City; it was and is to bring affordable fine food.

---

196 David Chang, "Season 1 Episode 1: Noodle," posted November 9, 2012 on PBS The Mind of a Chef, video, 23:10.

Ramen was just the first vehicle to do that. Chef Baca said it best, "People like us used to think that the only way to run a restaurant was the big model, the old school, the fine dining, and what Momo did was to break that mold."[197]

So how did Momofuku break that mold?

David Chang and Joaquin Baca did what they know best, use the techniques that they learned in fine dining to make delicious food.

First, they sourced the best ingredients. The braised pork slices in the bowls were made with Berkshire pork, which is the highest quality pork money can buy.[198] The corn that they garnish the ramen with is farm-fresh from Greenmarket, a Farmer's Market in Union Square that's been around since 1976 bringing together 140 vendors who offer only high-quality ingredients.[199]

Second, they leveled up the cooking techniques. Instead of making a soft-boiled egg which takes about six minutes in boiling water, they slow poached their eggs. This means they measure the temperature of the water to exactly 140 degrees Fahrenheit and then soak the eggs for forty to forty-five minutes at that temperature.[200]

---

[197] Maura Judkis, "Ramen, Noise and Rebellion," *Washington Post*, September 19, 2019.

[198] D'artagnan, "Food Fight: Berkshire Pork vs. Kurobuta Pork," *Center of the Plate* (blog), May 9, 2017.

[199] Patronite and Raisfeld, "The I Chang."

[200] Technokidz, "Momofuku Slow-Poached Eggs," *Epicurious*, updated September 24, 2015.

Third, they had the heavyweights of the restaurant industry come in to eat. This wasn't necessarily a business strategy that was intentional but by chance this is what put the restaurant over the top. Chang told this story once about how during the very beginnings of the restaurant, he had staff leaving all the time. And one day, his dishwasher never came in. Why is this important? Because if there are no clean dishes, nothing gets served. Dishwashing is a high-pressure job, you have to work quickly and accurately because there is no in between a clean and unclean plate. And, the stakes are high, a customer's health is at risk. That day, the absence of the dishwasher slowed down everything else in the restaurant that night. Luckily, it just so happened that a bunch of Chang's friends from Cafe Boulud came in to eat.

His chef friends from Cafe Boulud ended up "all washing dishes that night. I think what really carried us at the end of the day was that we really took care of the cooks. The word really spread."[201] They all loved the food, and, let's be honest, what's better publicity for a restaurant than a bunch of chefs enjoying the food? Nothing.

Fourth, the food was so affordable. How much do you think a bowl of ramen from Momofuku cost? $15? $18? No. Their bowl of ramen would set you back $7 to $11 for delicious food made with the best ingredients. For $7, what can the average American buy? One Big Mac, not even the meal. Maybe two coffees from Starbucks if you play your cards right. Or three-quarters of a Chipotle burrito bowl. However, you definitely can't get a full meal for $7.

---

201 Patronite and Raisfeld, "The I Chang."

Christina Tosi, the pastry chef that started Milk Bar, Momofuku's spin-off bakery, said it best, "He was making food for the people. He got out of fine dining on the savory side because he just wanted to make really good food that could reach more people and be more approachable."[202]

David Chang didn't just bring his version of ramen over from Japan, he brought over the idea of affordable fine dining. He thought that great food shouldn't be exclusive to the one percent of the world; he believed that everyone should have access to great food.

PRODUCT DEMOCRATIZATION
There is truly something lucrative about democratization. I know how ironic that sounds. Democratization is the act of making things accessible. So, what is lucrative about it? It is the fact that this concept has not become mainstream yet in the business world.

Think of any luxury product—Birken bags, Christian Louboutins, Glenlivet Scotch, Bentleys, and Michelin Star restaurants; truly the list could go on and on. If there is any common factor from all of these products, it is that they are all expensive, great quality, status symbols, and exclusive. We all know that there are cheaper alternatives to luxury goods—Madewell Bags, Nine West shoes, Johnnie Walker Red label, Kias, and McDonald's. But what differentiates these alternatives from their counterparts is the price and

---

[202] Maria Aspan, "How Milk Bar's Christina Tosi Went from Momofuku Employee to Bakery Chain CEO," *Inc.*, March/April 2018.

quality. To get from point A to point B, walking in Nine West pumps will walk you there just as fast as Christian Louboutins' stilettos, and a Kia could drive you there just as fast as a Bentley (assuming no speeding is involved). So why are people willing to pay tenfold the amount for one product when there is a cheaper alternative? Because we think it is of higher quality, made with better components, and can offer more units of happiness.

But what if that isn't true? What if we could get high-quality luxury products at the price of normal goods?

Some may say "That is impossible. You can't ensure the same experience or end product at such a low price; it wouldn't cover the cost."

David Chang didn't think so when he opened Momofuku. And I don't think so either.

David Chang might not have known the business term for what he was doing, but he was engaging in the process of democratization, allowing people access. Chang said, "Japan changed the way I think about food. It's a food culture. And food didn't have to be great on just a fine-dining level. You could eat really well. Even fast-food chains were awesome."[203]

The idea that consumers don't have to pay exorbitant prices for truly great products is a major step forward for equity inclusion and all the benefits that come from it, such as an expanded customer base, brand recognition, brand loyalty,

---

203 Patronite and Raisfeld, "The I Chang."

and a positive image. When you sell a great product or service at a great price, you are typically rewarded handsomely by your customers. I believe that when you can sell a great product or service at a price lower than your competitors, that's how you win. If you need an example, just look at Amazon.

So, how does an entrepreneur achieve a level of "democratization" for his or her product? Michael Wolf, Founder and Creator of Smart Kitchen Summit, an event combining technology and food, and former Forbes Contributor, outlined in a Forbes article "The 4 Pillars of Democratized Business":

1. Democratization of Knowledge: There is no better time for learning than right now. With the internet, any person, even a child, can learn how to gain actionable skills, like coding, on any number of learning platforms. In fact, MasterClass allows anyone with an account to learn from the experts: writing from Malcolm Gladwell, poker from Daniel Negreanu, cooking from Gordon Ramsey, or entrepreneurship from Howard Schultz to name just a few. When you learn, you gain skills. When you gain skills, you can do something with it. And if you do anything well enough, people will pay for it.[204]
2. Democratization of Creation: You don't need to spend crazy amounts of money to make something. You definitely do need some money to start with. But, it doesn't have to be a boatload. Wolf wrote about how "entrepreneurs no longer need to own the means of production

---

204 Michael Wolf, "The New Era of Democratized Business," *Forbes*, November 5, 2012.

but can now instead rent them" or about how they can use lower cost technologies and platforms to create their dreams. Entrepreneurs can find creative ways to access the inputs they need to create. Be scrappy and creative. I'll bring you back to Gordon Segal who chose to *rent* a retail space not even meant for furniture to sell luxury furniture. For a low cost up front, he was able to start earning enough profits for him to eventually buy the building, at a discount no less.[205]

3. Democratization of Funding: Between micro-loans, angel investors, crowdfunding, and any number of other options, businesses can get off the ground with limited capital. Venture capital and traditional commercial banking remain viable options for funding, but entrepreneurs now have so many other options to decide between to protect their best interests. For those not interested in losing equity, micro-loans can be just what you need to begin and sources of funding like Indiegogo and Kickstarter are the most democratized source of investing for investors on the market today. Entrepreneurs can tap into the power of the crowd nowadays to not only get funding but also gauge interest into the product. Every dollar invested from these crowdfunding sites is a vote of confidence in the demand of your product.[206]

4. Democratization of Distribution and Commerce: From a world once dominated by big retail, technology has put the power back into the entrepreneurs' hands. Craigslist, eBay, Depop, Shopify, Square, and many other online marketplaces are allowing single entrepreneurs and small

---

205 Ibid.
206 Ibid.

businesses alike to reach their customers without having to find a physical or traditional retail partner like the Walmarts and Amazons of the world. In fact, entrepreneurs can create their own e-commerce sites and directly reach their customers without having to pay retailers a thing.[207]

Each of these strategies can allow entrepreneurs to create a high-quality luxury good at a fraction of the price of their competitors. Customers know a great product when they see one, and the price tag is no longer the symbol of a great product. Alexa von Tobel, Managing Partner of Inspired Capital, CEO of LearnVest.com, a personal finance website, and champion of the democratization of products, has introduced a new concept of luxury, "I consider luxury products or services things that make my life easier, more seamless, enjoyable and consumable that were not necessarily available to the masses. So, they don't necessarily need to have a hefty price tag."[208]

So, how does Momofuku fit in? David Chang had the dream to sell fine-dining quality food at affordable prices. He set out to "make affordable good food, and do it with integrity."[209]

Chang utilized the democratization of creation in multiple ways. He chose low-cost ingredients from his local farmers market. To cut the cost of transportation of food ingredients,

---

207 Ibid.
208 Jeremy Goldman, "Why Brands Must Embrace the Democratization of Luxury in 2016," *Inc.*, January 4, 2016.
209 Patronite and Raisfeld, "The I Chang."

he walked to Greenmarket in Union Square to get the freshest ingredients he could get his hands on. Great food doesn't have to be made of expensive ingredients like caviar or truffle. What truly matters is the technique to elevate a food to the next level. David Chang and Joaquin Baca utilized fine dining techniques on humble ingredients to elevate the humble dish of ramen to new heights.

Anyone who is questioning whether this strategy worked need only know that he expanded Momofuku into an international empire with fifteen restaurants in three countries and six cities. Traveling the world from Japan to Europe helped open David Chang's eyes to the realities of food. Great food shouldn't be walled off to the wealthy; it should be shared with everyone. He decided to democratize food in America and the rest of the world.

CHAPTER 9

CONCLUSION

So, now we've talked about funding, retail partners, luxury branding, pivoting, monobrand structure, and democratization of products. Ultimately, this all boils down to relationships. Funding refers to your relationships with a bank, venture capitalists, or your close friends and family that help ensure financial success. Retail partnerships are a defining relationship with stores and marketplaces that can connect you to your customers. Luxury branding plays a huge role in your relationship with your customers and how you interact with them. Pivoting changes the relationship you have with your customers and must be dealt with carefully. Monobrand structure determines how your brand is looked at by your customers and retailers and suppliers and thus has many implications on how those relationships go. And democratization of products is a commitment to your customers, which builds on your relationships.

For an entrepreneur, the relationships you make with your customers, suppliers, financiers, and partners are critical to your business's success. Dr. Holly Schroth, an award-winning Senior Lecturer at UC Berkeley Haas School of Business who teaches Negotiations and Conflict Resolution, said, "I always believe in getting to know a person as a person, understanding their values and whether they align with yours, before you even consider doing business with them. I think the biggest mistake people do is they see relationships as transactions."

Every decision an entrepreneur makes starts with a relationship with someone else. And for an international business, there truly is nothing more important than building great relationships at home and abroad.

I want to bring you back to my first entrepreneurship idea: small bite-sized scrumptious chocolatey digestives. Now that I have my idea, it's time to execute. (And, maybe give you some ideas about how to implement some concepts for your own entrepreneurial ideas.)

Here's the idea for the short term:

FUNDING

I'm going to combine two options of funding: family/friends and crowdfunding. The great thing about selling a food product is that my up-front costs are minimized. The ingredients aren't expensive, only my time is. But, this is my brainchild and I love cooking and sharing that joy. I'll take a page from the three original founders of Starbucks' book who didn't quit their jobs to work full time on their entrepreneurship idea and do the same thing. Baking and packaging these chocolate-covered biscuits will take all of my time on the weekend and at night. All friends and family who invest in my business will be my testers who give me feedback on the digestives. My Kickstarter.com campaign will work the same way; everyone who invests will get shipped a batch of digestives and a handwritten thank you card from me. It's the perfect set up: I get funding and crucial potential customer feedback, and my investors get a batch of digestives which are sure to taste delicious.

PIVOTS

Some things are classics and can never be changed, like Coca Cola or Bohemian Rhapsody. Most other things are not classics, which means constant improvements and paying attention to trends are imperative to staying relevant as a brand. And if we have learned anything from Starbucks, it's that even something as classic as coffee beans can change into something even more revolutionary. These chocolate-covered biscuits will start off as exactly that, down-to-earth straightforward wheatmeal biscuits with a coating of milk chocolate. As new trends come out, different ingredients can be used to enhance this cookie. The last thing I would want is for something as dynamic and versatile as a food item to stay stagnant.

RETAIL

Starting off, I want to start selling chocolate-covered biscuits from my own social media accounts and making them to order. As I start receiving orders, I'll contact retailers and grocery stores like Trader Joe's and Safeway who I know already sell similar products. I'd like to get placement at the end of the checkout aisles in these stores next to the other small grab-and-go chocolate snacks. Instead of getting placement in an actual aisle where customers are more likely to reach for a familiar product, the check-out aisle is better because it's a quick decision where people are willing to take a chance on something new. Then, as I get established, I'll lay the groundwork to get placed in the big kahuna of retailers, Walmart, as this is the mark of a product that "made it." The same way Tatcha placed such an emphasis on getting stocked at Barneys, having my chocolate-covered biscuits picked up by a mainstream retailer is the mark of a successful product.

STRUCTURE

Following in April Gargiulo's footsteps, I know that one product can be enough. I'll focus on these chocolate-covered biscuits until the recipe is perfect and everyone else knows it too. A good quality product truly speaks for itself and customers will come back around to give feedback suggestions for new snacks to come out with.

DEMOCRATIZATION OF A PRODUCT

Snacks are not a luxury good, nor do I want my delicious chocolate-covered biscuits to become a luxury good. However, currently there is a higher cost associated with purchasing the British digestives from the US as anyone outside of the UK will have to pay for international shipping. This is because digestives are produced in the UK, and if you choose to get it shipped, you'll have to deal with a melted, stuck together, crumbly mess as it is literally shipped across the ocean. I don't want this either. Frankly, I want to share this delicious snack with everyone in the United States because it's a good thing, and something that brings value shouldn't be confined.

If I can hope for you to get two things out of this book, they are first that there are truly infinite sources of inspiration that are all around us and, second, the only way to find something new is to dive right into it. I now know that the Brits have been enjoying digestives for ages, and it's only just a relatively new concept to me. Without going across the pond, I would've never found out about my favorite snack or my next entrepreneurial idea. At the same time, Howard Schultz would have never started Starbucks without that first business trip to Italy. Dietrich Mateschitz would never have created Red Bull or his energy drink empire without flying to Thailand and trying a local drink.

Victoria Tsai would never have come across blotting papers or ancient Japanese skin care traditions without being exposed to them from her business trips for Starbucks. April Gargiulo would never have created Vintner's Daughter without visiting an apothecary in Morocco and taking a chance on face oil for the first time. Gordon and Carole Segal wouldn't have discovered the process of importing from European manufacturers without taking a honeymoon in the Caribbean Islands. Doug Ricket would have never known about the new electric system without seeing it in Ghana nor reinvented this idea to make pay-as-you-go smartphones. And David Chang would never have introduced his style of affordable fine dining or ramen without working in Japan as an English teacher.

So the next time you hop on a plane to a foreign land, take a page out of these business leaders and founder CEOs' books and keep your eyes peeled for the ways that people hundreds of miles away can be doing things, using things, eating things, and creating things better than what you know from home.

You never know what you might find, be inspired by, or reinvent. Before the CEOs in our books became *the CEOs*, they started off in the exact place you are in right now. If they can dream it, so can you.

BOOK ACKNOWLEDGMENTS

Throughout this book writing journey, I have learned that it takes a village. Here are the people I'd like to highlight in my village:

Ru Shi, Kaizan Huang, and Richard Huang, who have always believed that I can achieve anything I set my mind to.

Garrett Backer and Jessie Ko, who have always been there to celebrate a milestone and encourage me when I hit a wall. Our Facetimes and conversations are invaluable.

Elizabeth Minchilli, Alan Ross, Dan Himelstein, Monte Woods, Peter Molloy, and Holly Schroth, who were so generous with their time and minds to indulge me in an interview and offer me insights. Like a painting, this book is more colorful with your input.

Saumya Goyal, Christian Fong, Kai Zhao, Jessie Ko, Garrett Backer, Olivia Reinoso, Ingrid Chau, and Brian Kehoe, who have been so willing to give me constructive feedback and beta read one or more chapters of my book. They've pushed me to clarify cloudy concepts, expand on particular sections, and made me reexamine if what I wrote is what I want to say.

Amanda Munro and John Chancey, who have been the most incredible editors. Their detailed comments have driven my writing and taught me new ways to put the right words on paper.

Eric Koester, who was the first to believe in me and bring me on this journey.

New Degree Press, my publisher, who has been so supportive in getting this book to the finish line.

And all of my supporters without whom this book wouldn't be possible:

Shannon Kakuk, Engel Yue, Noelle Link, Saumya Goyal, Estefania Martinez Pardo, Christian Fong, Brian Kehoe, Kaizan Huang, Ingrid Chau, Eleanor Savas, Lanmei Luo, Xiaochun Dong, Olivia Reinoso, Jackie Sun, Dominick Carlson, Yingying Shu, Jianxin Shi, Shuai Wang, Xiaoxiao Chen, Dan Himelstein, Carly James, Tiffany Jing, Helen Wang, Liam Rahav, Gavin Levy, Helen Liu, Abby Regan, Ganqing Jiang, Peter Molloy, Austin Moon, Andrew Kilman, Jessie Ko, Isabella Impalli, Steffany Wong, Kanyi Huang, Simas Chacar-Palubinskas, Anthony Di Iorio, Alex Kaplan, Arlene Santiago, Eric Koester, Albert Hu, Matthew Teshome,

Charles Broussard, Puneet Sawhney, Winston Lau, Matthew Bradley, Akshara Dhadda, Daniel Tsentsiper, Danny Yim, Jennifer Backer, Matthew Schwarz, Joanne Wang, Andrea Buccino, Will Madden, Ricky Gilmore-Vega, Monte Wood, Olivia Wilkinson, Jose Solorzano, Lynna Harris, Katie Blake, Savanna Harwood, Andrew DiCandilo, Anthony Kim, Neha Dasari, Rena Yan, Goutham Swaminathan, Jeffrey Zhang, Derek Yao, Aki Kamoshida, Anna Shim, Ran Dan Pan, Jay Patel, Aaditya Mehta, Justin Oh, Derrick Luo, Charles Gooding, Nicholas Pedersen, Max Yang, Maureen Pescatore, Mary Kang, Gavin Lifrieri, Cecilia Yan, Liv Glassman, Angel Vu, Lion Raywood, Tiffany Huang, Jessica Lang, Anjana Prakasam, Skander Zmerli, Kai Chao, Kaushik Mahadevan, Nick Singh, Connor Aston, Adam Wolpert, Daniel Lee, Kevin Ma, Oren Mor, Paul Kaser, Ethan Park, Atina Schutz, Jonathan Leiberman, Hana Makota, Harrison Nicholas, Sabrina Dong, Josephine Wang, Caroline Chin, Michael Castellanos, Josue Vallecillo, Kabir Jain, Liz Schaeffer, Jennifer McGinty, Kyle Hayes, James Tramontana, Daniel Zhu, Jimmy Woods, Neil Ahluwalia, Lin Han, Lorenzo Cancel, Michael Grossman, Raksha Sen, Alexandra Dachenko, Michael Assadi, Jocelyn Greer, Kiran Abraham-Aggarwal, Renee Camarena, Daniella Stoltz, Garrett Backer, and Sarah Wang.

APPENDIX

INTRODUCTION

Berkeley Haas Alumni Network. "Scott Galloway—the Four." October 25, 2017. Video, 50:05. *http://www.youtube.com/ watch?v=n1xjdRRIzYw&t=2027s&ab_channel=BerkeleyHaas-AlumniNetwork.*

Farber, Dan. "What Steve Jobs Really Meant When He Said 'Good Artists Copy; Great Artists Steal'." *CNET*, January 28, 2014. *http://www.cnet.com/news/what-steve-jobs-really-meant-when-he-said-good-artists-copy-great-artists-steal/.*

Ignatius, Adi. "How Indra Nooyi Turned Design Thinking into Strategy: An Interview with PepsiCo's CEO." Harvard Business Review, September 2015. *http://hbr.org/2015/09/how-indra-nooyi-turned-design-thinking-into-strategy.*

CHAPTER 1

Cooperrider, David. "Sustainable Innovation." *BizEd*, July 1, 2008. *http://bized.aacsb.edu/articles/2008/07/sustainable-innovation#:~:text=Which%20brings%20us%20back%20to,must%20inevitably%20sacrifice%20financial%20performance.*

Hansen, Valerie. *The Silk Road: A New History*. Oxford: Oxford University Press, 2012.

CHAPTER 2: TATCHA

Abraham, Sitara. "6 Inspiring Quotes from Entrepreneurs about Business and Life." *Thought Catalog*, May 30, 2014. http://thoughtcatalog.com/sitara-abraham/2014/05/6-inspiring-quotes-from-entrepreneurs-about-business-and-life/.

Adalid, Aileen. "Geisha of Japan: Understanding the Facts, History & Myths." I Am Aileen, accessed August 18, 2020. https://iamaileen.com/geisha-facts-geiko-maiko/.

Blakely, Sara. "Build Awareness." Produced by Masterclass. *Masterclass*, accessed September 20, 2020. Video, 13:41. http://www.masterclass.com/classes/sara-blakely-teaches-self-made-entrepreneurship/chapters/pricing-positioning.

Cleveland Clinic. "Dermatitis." Last reviewed October 29, 2020. http://my.clevelandclinic.org/health/articles/4089-dermatitis.

GoodGuide. "13 Years Ago." Accessed October 6, 2020. https://goodguide.com/.

Helm, Burt. "How a Geisha's Secret Helped Me Found My Company." *Inc.*, September 2015. http://www.inc.com/magazine/201509/burt-helm/2015-inc5000-memoirs-of-a-wannabe-geisha.html.

Jones, Geoffrey G., and Veronica Tang. "Tatcha: Marketing the Beauty Secrets of Japanese Geisha." *Harvard Business Review*, June 21, 2016. http://hbsp.harvard.edu/product/313149-HCB-ENG.

Kelley Blue Book. Kelley Blue Book Brand Watch: Luxury Segment Topline Report. Irvine, CA., accessed October

21, 2020. http://d2n8sg27e5659d.cloudfront.net/wp-content/uploads/2019/08/2019Q2-Brand-Watch-Luxury-Topline.pdf/.

Liao, Christina. "An Inside Peek at Kyoto's Secretive Geisha Culture." *Vogue*, March 21, 2017. http://www.vogue.com/article/geisha-culture-kyoto-japan-how-to-see-geiko-maiko.

Rao, Priya. "Tatcha's Victoria Tsai: 'Love Your Clients, Love Your Products, Everything Else Is Icing.'" *The Glossy Beauty Podcast*. Produced by Glossy. Podcast, 27:39. http://open.spotify.com/episode/4sJJibZRYxE2NER6hE6uTy?si=tYEj66DtQBu_BIfit-azkw.

Raz, Guy. "Tatcha: Victoria Tsai." In *How I Built This* with Guy Raz. Produced by NPR. Podcast, 1:20:03. http://open.spotify.com/episode/7v00e5ux8zM2KR3IWeIwuP?si=IiNTJmUIRmSvBloRnOoF5A.

Robin, Marci. "Beauty Giant Unilever Just Bought Tatcha for an Estimated $500 Million." *Allure*, June 11, 2019. http://www.allure.com/story/unilever-buys-tatcha-estimated-valuation.

CHAPTER 3: RED BULL

Appel, Tom. "What Was the Red Bull Car?" The Daily Drive, accessed August 30, 2020. http://blog.consumerguide.com/red-bull-car/.

Berger, Gerhard. "Brief Encounter: The Story of Gerhard Berger and Red Bull." *The Red Bulletin,* March 7, 2020. http://www.redbull.com/int-en/theredbulletin/f1-legend-gerhard-berger-letter.

Brown, David. "Red Bull vs Monster—Get Your Wings." November 13, 2018. In *Business Wars*. Produced by Wondery. Podcast, 26:00. http://podcasts.apple.com/us/podcast/business-wars/id1335814741?i=1000423753857.

Brynes, Sholto. The Independent. "Dietrich Mateschitz: Raging Bull." Accessed July 19, 2020. http://www.independent.co.uk/news/people/profiles/dietrich-mateschitz-raging-bull-17927.html.

Coetzee, Kristy. "Krating Daeng: Thailand's Original Red Bull Energy Drink." Slumber Party Hostels, accessed August 30, 2020. http://slumberpartyhostels.com/thai-red-bull-origins/.

Farris, Paul, Ervin Shames, Richard Johnson, and Jordan Mitchell. Red Bull in Brief. Charlottesville, VA: University of Virginia—Darden School of Business, 2016. Accessed August 30, 2020. http://faculty.darden.virginia.edu/farrisp/jnjcourseii/general/documents/redbullm-0663_condensed.pdf.

Jones, Robert. *Branding: A Very Short Introduction*. Oxford: Oxford University Press, 2017.

Mawer, Rudy. "What Is Taurine? Benefits, Side Effects and More." Healthline, accessed July 23, 2020. https//www.healthline.com/nutrition/what-is-taurine.

McDonald, Duff. "Red Bull's Billionaire Maniac Becomes a Media Mogul." NBC News, accessed July 19, 2020. http://www.nbcnews.com/id/wbna43112711#.XxTOu_hKi3K.

Moore, Kaleigh. "Red Bull's Approach to Marketing: Then and Now." Banknotes, accessed August 30, 2020. http://hashtagpaid.com/banknotes/red-bulls-approach-to-marketing-then-and-now.

O'Connor Claire. "US Specialized Industry Report OD4205: Energy Drink Production." Accessed August 30, 2020, IBISWorld.

Rodgers, Anni L. "It's a (Red) Bull Market after All." Fast Company, accessed August 30, 2020. http://www.fastcompany.com/64658/its-red-bull-market-after-all.

Souza, John. "10 Best Quotes from Seth Godin on PR and Marketing." Social Media Impact, April 10, 2014. http://www.socialmediaimpact.com/top-10-best-quotes-seth-godin-pr-marketing/#.

CHAPTER 4: VINTNER'S DAUGHTER

Blakely, Sara. "Build Awareness." Produced by Masterclass. *Masterclass*, accessed September 20, 2020. Video, 13:41. http://www.masterclass.com/classes/sara-blakely-teaches-self-made-entrepreneurship/chapters/build-awareness.

Czech, Joanna. "April Gargiulo." Joanna Czech, accessed September 14, 2020. http://www.joannaczech.com/blogs/czechlist/vintner-s-daughter-founder-april-gargiulo.

Dalton, Amy N., and Stephen A. Spiller. "Too Much of a Good Thing: The Benefits of Implementation Intentions Depend on the Number of Goals." *Journal of Consumer Research 39*, no. 3 (2012): 600-14. Accessed October 21, 2020. http://doi.org/10.1086/664500.

Johnson, Kirbie, and Sara Tan. "How Wine Inspired a Cult-Favorite Serum with April Gargiulo from Vintner's Daughter." In *Gloss Angeles*, produced by Kirbie Johnson, podcast, 46:39. http://www.listennotes.com/podcasts/gloss-angeles/how-wine-inspired-a-cult-GnjbTYcf5qe/.

Lewis, Victoria. "The Face Oil to End All Face Oils." *INTO THE GLASS*, accessed September 14, 2020. http://intothegloss.com/2015/03/vintners-daughter-serum/.

Sagansky, Gillian. "How a Former Winemaker Ended Up Making Gwyneth Paltrow's Go-To Serum." *W Magazine*, accessed August 9, 2020. https://www.wmagazine.com/story/vintners-daughter-serum-skincare/.

Snyder, Danielle. "Minimal Skincare, Maximum Impact | No Filter Ep. 11 Vintner's Daughter." In *No Filter* with Danielle Snyder. Produced by Danielle Snyder. Podcast, 36:00. https://open.spotify.com/episode/3OljynK7WcdvZRtKu6m8iX?si=4LV-jUmMUS--xOiral7aLoQ.

Vintner's Daughter. "Active Botanical Serum." Accessed August 9, 2020. http://vintnersdaughter.com/products/active-botanical-serum.

CHAPTER 5: PAYJOY

Lawanson, Jumoke. "'Our Goal Is to Deliver Access to Smartphone Financing Technology.'" *Business Day*, November 12, 2019. https://businessday.ng/technology/article/our-goal-is-to-deliver-access-to-smartphone-financing-technology/.

Farr, Sheila. "Starbucks: The Early Years." HistoryLink.org, February 15, 2017. http://www.historylink.org/File/20292.

Heaslip, Emily. "9 Wildly Successful Crowdfunded Startups." CO, published October 1, 2019. http://www.uschamber.com/co/start/startup/successful-crowdfunded-startups.

Irrera, Anna. "U.S. Smartphone Financing Tech Startup Payjoy Raises $20 Million." *Reuters*, May 23, 2019. http://www.reuters.com/article/us-payjoy-funding/u-s-smartphone-financing-tech-startup-payjoy-raises-20-million-idUSKCN1ST1JP.

JPMorgan Chase & Co. "How Momofuku's David Chang Turned His Dream into a Global Food Brand." Accessed October 12, 2020. http://www.jpmorganchase.com/news-stories/how-david-chang-turned-his-dream-into-global-food-brand.

Koren, James R. "Got No Credit? PayJoy Will Finance Your Phone—but Turn It into a Brick If You Don't Pay." *Hartford*

Courant, December 2, 2016. http://www.courant.com/la-fi-payjoy-phone-lock-20161202-story.html.

Rappaport, Sarah. "Kickstarter Funding Brings 'Veronica Mars' Movie to Life." *CNBC*, March 12, 2014. http://www.cnbc.com/2014/03/12/kickstarter-funding-brings-veronica-mars-movie-to-life.html.

Patel, Sujan. "21 Success Tips for Young and Aspiring Entrepreneurs." *Entrepreneur*, accessed February 8, 2021. http://www.entrepreneur.com/article/247540#:~:text=Have%20a%20vision.,vision%20clear%20at%20all%20times.

Schultz, Howard. "Find the Right Investors." Produced by Masterclass. *Masterclass*, accessed October 13, 2020. Video, 0:13. http://www.masterclass.com/classes/howard-schultz-leading-a-values-based-business/chapters/find-the-right-investors#.

Shieber, Jonathan. "With $4.3 Million PayJoy Is Ensuring Smartphones Land in the Hands of the Next 2 Billion." *Tech Crunch*, December 18, 2015. http://techcrunch.com/2015/12/18/with-4-3-million-payjoy-is-ensuring-smartphones-land-in-the-hands-of-the-next-2-billion/.

Sidney, G. "Restaurant Failure Rates Recounted: Where Do They Get Those Numbers?" RestaurantOwner.com, accessed October 12, 2020. http://www.restaurantowner.com/public/Restaurant-Failure-Rates-Recounted-Where-Do-They-Get-Those-Numbers.cfm.

Sutton, Danielle. "The Ultimate Introductory Guide to Funding Your Social Enterprise." Acumen Academy (blog), Acumen Academy, July 27, 2019. http://www.acumenacademy.org/blog/impact-capital-funding-your-social-enterprise.

TechTycoons. "Doug Ricket." Accessed August 6. http://techtycoons.com/doug-ricket/.

The Body Shop. "Our Activism." Accessed October 13, 2020. *http:// www.thebodyshop.com/en-us/about-us/activism/a/a00015.*

Turner, Ash. "How Many Smartphones Are in the World?" Bank-MyCell (blog), BankMyCell, accessed September 19, 2020. *http://www.bankmycell.com/blog/how-many-phones-are-in-the-world.*

CHAPTER 6: CRATE & BARREL

Gurzki, Hannes. "Dreaming up a World—How Luxury Brands Create Desire." *Forbes*, November 20, 2019. *http://www.forbes.com/sites/esmtberlin/2019/11/20/dreaming-up-a-world--how-luxury-brands-create-desire/amp/.*

Khan, Joseph P. "Crate & Barrel in 1985: A Startup on Display." *Inc.*, November 1, 1985. *http://www.inc.com/magazine/19851101/1328.html.*

Morzine Avoriaz. "Meet Gerard the Potter." Accessed September 11, 2020. *http://en.morzine-avoriaz.com/meet-gerard-the-potter.html.*

PegaseBuzz. "Hermès—Bandanas de soie [Commercial 2014]." July 11, 2014. Video, 1:30. *http://www.youtube.com/watch?v=XWX-4OQ04-Ns&ab_channel=PegaseBuzz.*

Raz, Guy. "Crate & Barrel: Gordon Segal." In *How I Built This* with Guy Raz. Produced by NPR. Podcast, 31:38. *http://open.spotify.com/episode/6DXbD29k3KS1gsXjt2GNTe?si=L-1xOn-3VRkSv9WqCa7l4cw.*

Silverstein, Michael J., and Neil Fiske. "Luxury for the Masses." *Harvard Business Review*, April, 2003. *http://hbr.org/2003/04/luxury-for-the-masses.*

CHAPTER 7: STARBUCKS

Biography.com Editors. "Howard Schultz Biography." *A&E Television Networks*, updated September 9, 2019. http://www.biography.com/business-figure/howard-schultz.

Farr, Sheila. "Starbucks: The Early Years." HistoryLink.org, February 2, 2017. http://www.historylink.org/File/20292.

Goodreads. "Quotable Quote." Accessed August 26, 2020. http://www.goodreads.com/quotes/76288-travel-makes-one-modest-you-see-what-a-tiny-place.

Hook. "How a Poor Kid from Brooklyn Made Starbucks." March 2, 2020. Video, 8:30. http://youtu.be/8-N3VqOmqPA.

Knowledge@Wharton. "When and How Entrepreneurs Pivot." *Knowledge@Wharton*, June 11, 2019. http://knowledge.wharton.upenn.edu/article/pivot-entrepreneurship/.

Poggioli, Sylvia. "Italy's Coffee Culture Brims with Rituals and Mysterious Rules." *NPR*, July 14, 2017. http://www.npr.org/sections/thesalt/2017/07/14/535638587/italys-coffee-culture-brims-with-rituals-and-mysterious-rules.

Raz, Guy. "Live Episode! Starbucks: Howard Schultz." In *How I Built This* with Guy Raz, produced by NPR, podcast, 49:42. http://open.spotify.com/episode/3Toatk9VPcwZ9ht1AygEYc?si=c1g5PdgDSdGqFqB4sWyoPQ.

The Corp With A-Rod and Big Cat. "Howard Schultz Talks Starbucks, Baseball, and Supersonics with A-Rod & Barstool Big Cat—The Corp." September 24, 2019. Video, 1:09:32. http://youtu.be/jflhhhkKCHg.

CHAPTER 8: MOMOFUKU

Aspan, Maria. "How Milk Bar's Christina Tosi Went from Momofuku Employee to Bakery Chain CEO." *Inc.*, March/April 2018. http://www.inc.com/magazine/201804/maria-aspan/christina-tosi-milk-bar-momofuku-bakery.html.

Chang, David. "On Guts." Open Transcripts at Patreon, August 25, 2013. http://opentranscripts.org/transcript/on-guts/.

Chang, David. "Season 1 Episode 1: Noodle." Posted November 9, 2012 on PBS *The Mind of a Chef*, video, 23:10. http://www.pbs.org/video/mind-chef-mind-chef-episode-1-noodle/.

D'artagnan. "Food Fight: Berkshire Pork vs. Kurobuta Pork." Center of the Plate (blog), May 9, 2017. http://center-of-the-plate.com/2017/05/09/food-fight-berkshire-pork-vs-kurobuta-pork/.

Goldman, Jeremy. "Why Brands Must Embrace the Democratization of Luxury in 2016." *Inc.*, January 4, 2016. http://www.inc.com/jeremy-goldman/why-brands-must-embrace-the-democratization-of-luxury-in-2016.html.

InterNations Go! "The Cost of Living in Japan." Updated April 21, 2020. http://www.internations.org/go/moving-to-japan/living/the-cost-of-living-in-japan.

Judkis, Maura. "Ramen, Noise and Rebellion." *Washington Post*, September 19, 2019. http://www.washingtonpost.com/graphics/2019/lifestyle/food/david-chang/.

Krestyn, Anna. "What Is the via Negativa?" Aleteia, March 4, 2013. http://aleteia.org/2013/03/04/what-is-the-via-negativa/.

Patronite, Rob, and Robin Raisfeld. "The I Chang." New York, January 12, 2007. http://nymag.com/restaurants/features/26568/.

Patel, Sujan. "21 Success Tips for Young and Aspiring Entrepreneurs." *Entrepreneur*, accessed February 8, 2021. *http://www.entrepreneur.com/article/247540*

Shepard, Dax. "David Chang." In *Armchair Expert* with Dax Shepard. Produced by Armchair Umbrella. Podcast, 1:38:31. *http://open.spotify.com/episode/35CIFPSuFRyKQuwnNo-8J7O?si=K6ynFhb9TliJPgpf6oD42Q.*

Tan, Alethea. "10 Types of Ramen and Where They Are From." *Michelin Guide Singapore*, October 2, 2017. *http://guide.michelin.com/sg/en/article/features/know-your-ramen-10-types-and-where-they-come-from.*

Technokidz. "Momofuku Slow-Poached Eggs." *Epicurious*, updated September 24, 2015. *http://www.epicurious.com/recipes/member/views/momofuku-slow-poached-eggs-52212401.*

Wolf, Michael. "The New Era of Democratized Business." *Forbes*, November 5, 2012. *http://www.forbes.com/sites/michaelwolf/2012/11/05/the-new-era-of-democratized-business/?sh=2d-2c767e8dd1.*

www.ingramcontent.com/pod-product-compliance
Lightning Source LLC
LaVergne TN
LVHW011829060526
838200LV00053B/3958